THE
BEAUTIFUL
UNSEEN

THE BEAUTIFUL UNSEEN

VARIATIONS ON FOG AND FORGETTING

A MEMOIR

KYLE BOELTE

SOFT SKULL PRESS / BERKELEY / AN IMPRINT OF COUNTERPOINT

Library of Congress Cataloging-in-Publication Data Is Available

ISBN 978-1-61902-458-8

Cover design by Debbie Berne
Interior Design by Neuwirth & Associates

Counterpoint Press
2560 Ninth Street, Suite 318
Berkeley, CA 94710
www.counterpointpress.com

Printed in the United States of America
Distributed by Publishers Group West

10 9 8 7 6 5 4 3 2 1

ACKNOWLEDGMENTS

Chapter 1: Quotes with permission from *For the Time Being*, by Annie Dillard. Published by Vintage/Random House.

Chapter 5 originally appeared, in a slightly different form, in *Lost Magazine*.

Chapter 11: "Suburban Denver School Trying To Halt The Rise In LSD Use," used with permission of The Associated Press. Copyright © 2014. All rights reserved.

Chapter 13: Quotes with permission from *Come Out and Play*. Words by Bryan Keith Holland.

Chapter 36: Quotes with permission from *Hey You*. Words and Music by Roger Waters. © 1979 Roger Waters Overseas Ltd. All Rights in the U.S. and Canada Administered by Warner-Tamerlane Publishing Corp. All Rights Reserved.

Chapter 36: Excerpt from *The Bridge of San Luis Rey* by Thornton Wilder. Copyright ©1927 by The Wilder Family LLC. Licensed by arrangement with The Wilder Family LLC and The Barbara Hogenson Agency, Inc. All rights reserved.

Chapter 40: Quotes with permission from *LSD: My Problem Child*, by Albert Hofmann. Used with permission by Multidisciplinary Association for Psychedelic Studies (MAPS).

Harold Gilliam's *Weather of the San Francisco Bay Region* (University of California Press) was an indispensible reference.

FOR MOM AND DAD

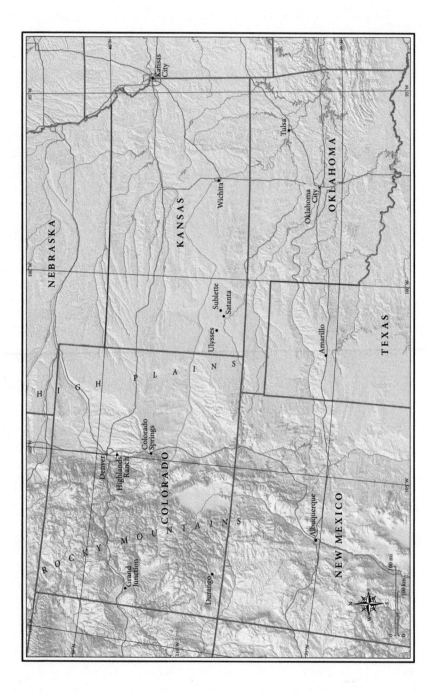

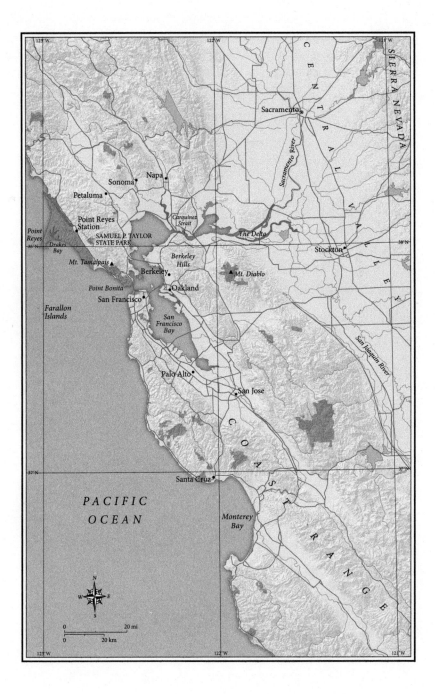

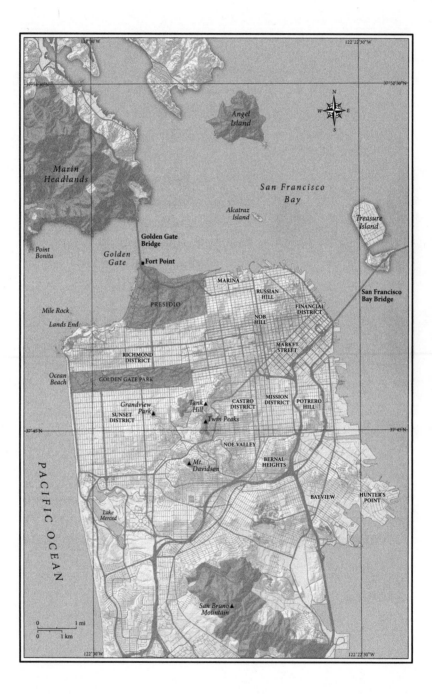

Forgetting belongs to all action, just as not only light but also darkness belong in the life of all organic things.

—FRIEDRICH NIETZSCHE
Basel, Switzerland

And further, this past is much affected by the present moment.

—VIRGINIA WOOLF
Monks House, England

Then the whole fascinating vision vanished, enveloped in cloud once more.

—NOEL ODELL
North Ridge, Everest

THE
BEAUTIFUL
UNSEEN

1

I DO NOT BELIEVE in ghosts. I am generally skeptical of the immaterial, the spiritual, the otherworldly. And yet, when I am by myself in the house at night—most any house, if alone—I often look up half expecting my brother Kris to be there. Across the room, hanging, often hanging, though I do not know what that would look like precisely. It is a vague vision—what is seeing?—no doubt pulled from movies or photographs glimpsed and then mostly forgotten.

The world outside is dark beyond the windowpane. Inside, the lights are on. All of them.

I read a book, arranging myself on the couch so that my back is to the wall and I am facing the hallway to the stairs that lead to the basement. I hear the house shift as the temperature drops, a groan from the floorboards. A phantom walking up the stairs.

I look up from my book and scan the room.

When I get up for a glass of water, I make sure not to walk with my back exposed to—to what? I'm not sure. I reassure myself that Kris would never want to harm me. Would never want to scare me, even. Is it Kris, then, who I sense? Why does my mind insist on frightening me with things better left for a thirteen-year-old child? I am now almost twice as old as Kris ever was.

I return to my book. I hold it—physical, real—in my hands. I believe in dirt, skin, tears, rock, blood, sky. I know the cold of water when I step into a mountain stream. When I encounter granite, or basalt, or sandstone on a hike, I touch it and feel it rough against my skin. I hold the book in my hands and begin to read again.

A few years ago, I grew interested in sand. Why is there sand in deserts? Where does it come from? I thought ocean waves made sand on seashores: waves pounded continents' rock and shattered it to stone, gravel, and finally sand. This, I learned, is only slightly true.

The house continues to groan. The heat kicks on. I look up again. I scan the room.

Clay particles clump and lie low; sand grains part and blow about. Winds drop sand by weight, as one drops anything when it gets too heavy for one's strength.

At some point the night must end and I must put down the book. I brush my teeth in the bathroom, leaving the door open. When I have finished, I walk through the hall past the stairs and into the bedroom. I turn on the light by the bed. I walk back out into the hall, where I glance down the stairs, looking without looking, before turning off the overhead light and heading back into the illuminated bedroom. I shut the door.

When I lived with roommates, the house was rarely empty at night. And now, in the house I share with Julia, I do not think twice about the dark when she is here—with the possible exception of the base-ment—but when she is gone, at a conference or visiting her parents in D.C., I begin to see the things I know are not there.

I lie down, turn off the bedside light, and pull the blanket over my head until morning.

2

FOR DAYS THE SHIP sailed into strong headwinds and across high seas. It had disembarked from Hong Kong, bound for San Francisco with a brief stopover in Honolulu. By the time it neared California, the ship was two days behind schedule. As it approached the coast, the crew and passengers of the SS *City of Rio de Janeiro* strained their eyes looking into the blue-gray haze with anticipation.

It was February 20, 1901. Everyone's thoughts that morning were occupied with a longing for land. They wanted first just to see it, to know that something solid outside of this frantic sea existed. Once they saw it—once they knew it to be real and not another mirage floating off in the distance—they would long to stand on it, to feel the world solid beneath their feet.

They stared into the haze all morning, into the gray of distance stretching forever out in front of them. Then, at midmorning, they could see it. Out beyond the haze was a thin strip of blue on the horizon. Land.

Their relief didn't last long. Just four miles off shore, a sea of fog engulfed the ship. The skipper ordered the anchor down. They would wait for clear weather. Again the passengers and crew stood looking out onto a blank canvas. One was a father-to-be who was hoping to discover that his child had been born. Another was the U.S. consul general to Hong Kong, along with his wife and son. Once the ship made landfall, they planned to catch a train across the continent to attend President McKinley's inauguration. All told, there were 211 on board. They waited together in the thick fog, swaying in the sea just a few miles from solid ground.

Captain William Ward paced the fog-filled deck. He had a fiancée who was waiting for him in San Francisco. He had not seen her in some time, and now the only thing that stood between him and her was this thick fog that he could not see past. The anchor chains creaked under strain. The ship's fog bell rang out every thirty seconds to warn nearby vessels of the *Rio*'s presence. No others were nearby. The *Rio* was alone at anchor in the gray fog.

"Before every great shipwreck there is a single crucial moment when an immediate and final decision must be made," Harold Gilliam notes in his book *San Francisco Bay*. "Once that moment is passed, no further choice is possible."

Everything is in control. The boat is steady. Life is manageable. The future is a placid sea stretching into the distance. The sky is clear. The harbor just a couple of miles ahead. Then a final decision. A fog forms. Control slips away. The world is a wilderness once more.

In the late afternoon, a small pilot boat appeared from behind the fog. Unable to see, it had followed the ringing of the ship's fog bell. The *Rio* lowered a rope ladder and pilot Fred W. Jordan climbed aboard, ready to guide the ship into port. He brought with him a stack of newspapers. The passengers, isolated from the outside world, eagerly grabbed for one. They began to speak more quickly. Anticipation blossomed into excitement. They could almost feel the land beneath their feet as they read the day's news. The father-to-be flipped to the back of the paper. He had become the father of a baby boy. He passed around his last few cigars.

Soon enough, San Franciscans would be reading about the *Rio*'s tragic end.

That evening, the fog began to thin, and the captain, tired of waiting, ordered the anchor up. The *Rio* once more headed east, slowly, tentatively, approaching the Golden Gate Strait. It did not make it far. Fog again appeared, an apparition that swallowed the ship. The anchor was lowered once more.

Captain Ward's frustration transformed into disgust. He stormed off the deck and into his cabin. He was to be summoned only once the fog lifted. Until then, he would sleep. The ship rocked through the night, alone in its own world, the anchor creaking, the fog bell ringing, the fog hanging heavy over the sleeping passengers.

Then, at four in the morning, the pilot saw a clearing in front of the ship. He rubbed sleep from his eyes and looked landward where he saw the flickering lights of the Fort Point and Point Bonita lighthouses. Captain Ward was awoken, as were the ship's engines.

The *Rio* cautiously approached the Golden Gate, moving slowly through the deep channel. Then, at once, it entered a patch of fog— the few who were awake held their breath—only to escape it within minutes. A false alarm; the crew let out a collective exhale. The ship passed Lands End and Mile Rock. They could almost feel the land within grasp. The lighthouse at Point Bonita slid behind the stern as the ship entered the strait, and the world of land in front of them opened up.

The passengers slept as the SS *City of Rio de Janeiro* approached the narrows, on the edge of San Francisco, in the year nineteen hundred and one, where it was engulfed one final time in a wall of fog.

3

NINE HUNDRED FEET ABOVE the sea, atop Eureka Peak, the fog blows in. Ever changing, it hurries past, relentlessly at times, wave after wave.

It's a long walk up from Market Street, and a world away from the crowded bars in the Castro. Past the neon signs and Victorian houses, up steep streets and then hidden stairways, up, up, up the small footpaths that wind across the ridges, across Scenic Drive and then up another short stretch of trail: Twin Peaks. Noe and Eureka.

To the east, the city proper, beyond the fog's reach but framed by it. The procession of cars on Market Street cuts straight through downtown, ending only where the San Francisco Bay begins. North of Market: Russian Hill, Nob Hill, and the Financial District. South of Market: the Mission, Potrero Hill, and Bernal Heights. In the distance, the Bay Bridge reaches out to Oakland.

Across the crowded city, people come and go. Buses and trains trace their prescribed lines. On the highway, red taillights back up to the Bay Bridge. People are everywhere living their lives, a frantic mass of energy. I look out at all that movement, all those lives I will never know except for the blur of light I see from this peak, and pause.

Concentrate on just one life.

Up here, in the middle of San Francisco, only a few people are to be found. This city has many pockets of quiet amid the din of urban life. Solitude and space for contemplation.

A moment later, the wind changes, and the fog begins to move in on it all. The city and people and buses and cars—all of it down there—disappear in the fog. I am enveloped by it, left alone in the fog atop this peak.

I turn around. The wind and the fog both originate to the west, where the ocean meets the land. The fog is denser out there, the city sleepier. From Eureka Peak, at times you cannot see much to the west past where you stand. At your feet, elderberry, and arroyo willow, and reed grass, and rock. Beyond the fog, if you believe in what you cannot see, lies the Richmond District, Golden Gate Park, Ocean Beach, the Sunset District, and the Pacific Ocean stretching westward. The sun, out beyond the Sunset, is setting high in the sky above a bank of fog that swallows up the land.

· · ·

I'VE BEEN THINKING ABOUT fog for some time now. How it appears outside my window in the morning while I'm lying in bed, the outside world neither dark nor light. How it moves along the streets like a thousand streams tracing the contours of the city. How it obscures the world, confusing the seen and unseen. And then, how it slowly disappears from sight until the world is once again visible.

Memory is like the fog. I remember feeling for the first time, as a teenager, what it was like to forget. How something so concrete could one day disappear. I remarked to a friend that I no longer knew the sound of a voice I once knew so well. The forgetting has stuck with me.

And yet, for all the forgetting, much remains. Sorting it out is like walking through the fog in search of some distant part of the city. At times the past is illuminated, burning, brilliant. Other times the fog is thick. Often, it is just silently slipping away.

Standing, as it were, amid the fog, I sketch the landscape. Sometimes I'm able to see things fairly clearly. Often, much of my view is obscured. At times I must rely on others when I cannot see past my own feet. Simple sketches are all I can manage. Thoreau and

Dillard have their "meteorological journal of the mind." I have a fog sketchbook.

Memory is real, I've come to think, though it is living. The past mixes with the present—an endless churning. The fog swirls around so that this is visible, and then this is visible, and then this is visible.

· · ·

I USED TO LIVE in the heart of the fog, in the Sunset, off Irving Street, a couple of blocks from Golden Gate Park. The place was an old Edwardian, built two years after the 1906 quake, and the single-pane windows let the wind and fog right in. The building had made it through many earthquakes, but it hadn't seen much handiwork for a couple of decades. The linoleum floor in the kitchen was peeling off, as was the white paint in every room. My room was in the back of the house and my window faced west. On clear days I could almost see the ocean just a few miles away.

There weren't many clear days. The summer months were filled with fog. Wispy white fog. Thick gray fog. Fog that stood still and fog that blew sideways. I woke up to it in the mornings as it worked its way past the window frame. I would stand at a streetcar stop on Irving, waiting for the inbound N-Judah, and watch the fog flow toward me, an endless white river tumbling up the street. Downtown, after work, I would board the outbound N in sunshine, and, after passing through the Sunset Tunnel, the train would often emerge into a sea of fog.

I'm no expert when it comes to fog. I know it comes in from the west, from the ocean, and blows into the city. Summer, when temperatures just a hundred miles inland are in the nineties and above, is fog season here—cool and windy and sometimes downright cold. Some people I know run from the fog, leaving town each summer weekend to find sunshine in neighboring counties. And though I grew up in

Colorado, where any resident will tell you about the state's three hundred days of sunshine a year, I've grown to like the fog.

When I moved in with Julia, I moved to Bernal Heights, to the east of Twin Peaks, on the edge of the fog. Many of our neighbors live here specifically to stay away from it. Bernal lies in something of a banana belt, as most of the fog never makes it past Twin Peaks. But even when it is sunny in this part of town, the fog is often still present. Just look up toward Twin Peaks, where it streams down the leeward side into the Castro like head overflowing a pint of beer.

I've kept an eye on it, up there, to the west, atop the peaks. In spring, I sometimes return from an after-work run up Bernal Hill and tell Julia about the formations gathering in the Golden Gate. She smiles a knowing smile, indulges me a little, as if clouds have some real significance. I might then head up Twin Peaks, where the air is refreshingly cool, for no better reason than to feel it moving in against my skin.

I've started taking walks across the city in search of fog. These walks sometimes turn into long hikes. Up the green grass hills and through the city streets. I've found out-of-the-way staircases that lead deeper into it. I bought a pocket guide to Bay Area weather and I carry it with me as I walk. I sometimes search for scientific studies about fog online and read them at work when things are slow.

I've been living with the fog for some time now, surrounded, without knowing much about it. It's time I take a look around.

4

WHEN I THINK OF Kris, he is older than me still. In my mind I see brown hair, square shoulders, that he is tall. If asked to describe what he looked like, I would not be able to offer much more than that vague triad. I do not see details beyond that. When I see Kris, I *sense* someone older than me. The seeing and the sensing overlap. I do not know what the sensing is, simply that I feel it. As I grow older, Kris grows older too. He is my older brother still. We age together at a constant rate. Or, perhaps, when I think of him, I become younger.

. . .

THE SUBURB WE GREW up in had a series of greenbelts: preserved land flowing like inlets between the thousands of tract homes that stretched ever south from Denver. Highlands Ranch had been a cattle ranch in the not-so-distant past, and cattle still grazed on some of the land in 1991—a comfortingly pastoral sight for the seventeen thousand inhabitants of the ten-year-old suburban outpost.

When I was nine, a tall redheaded kid from the neighborhood and I would spend hours exploring our greenbelt. We spent most of our time down by the creek, protected from the hot summer sun by towering cottonwood trees. We would pack provisions and wander the great expanse just as Stephen Harriman Long had in July of 1820. His namesake peak (14,259 feet tall) looms over the Front Range, and under its watchful gaze we delighted in finding quicksand, and frogs, and the occasional owl. We shot at one with a BB gun once and it stoically stood its ground. We dreamed of finding swimming holes and stringing up rope swings that would propel us through the air and into the cool water below.

The greenbelt was true wilderness to us. We had no interest in definitions or boundaries—for us, the natural and the human flowed into each other. The houses on each side became cliffs towering above a gorge. We had no idea that suburban planners and marketers valued the greenbelt mostly as a "recreation area" to attract young families. A place where moms and dads could go for a run after a long day at the office. A place where they could turn their kids loose in summer without the fears of urban living. A place that reassured: development and conservation can live together—if at a ratio of one hundred to one.

On summer afternoons in Colorado, storm clouds formed near Longs Peak and neighboring mountains, where we could see them building, their strength growing. Then, as if given permission, they advanced across the plains, a torrent of rain and thunder and lightning. In the cities and suburbs, water gathered in the streets, the contours of the concrete forcing it through gutters to storm drains, where it disappeared into the underworld.

Once, just down from the greenbelt entrance, we found a storm drain outlet hidden behind the cottonwoods, around a bend in the creek. It was a large concrete block with a stream of water flowing from an opening at its base. We scaled the exterior wall above the opening and looked down into a room. After scoping out the obstacles inside, we decided to jump down. We waded five feet through ankle-deep water and climbed over a giant interior concrete wall to reach the farthest chamber, where a large drainpipe emerged. It was like nothing we had seen before, outside of *Super Mario Brothers*. Deep inside, the drainpipe was utterly dark, an emptiness from which a cool breeze blew.

....

"Because it's there," George Mallory said of climbing Everest. Our answer, at nine, to the question "Why do you want to enter the drainpipe?" would have been the same. Mallory was last seen a couple hundred meters from the summit of Everest in 1924. He was thirty-seven. His well-preserved body was found in 1999 on the North Face, at 26,760 feet. His partner's body was never found. We hadn't heard of either of them.

We went home to plan. We did not know what the pipe was exactly or why it was there. We did not know how long it was or if in fact it ever ended. We did know that we needed more provisions for this expedition, our most daring to date. We loaded up on flashlights, candles, matches, and Hostess CupCakes. Our load seemed heavy; never before had we carried so much. So we tied a rope to a skateboard and pulled our gear behind us.

When we got to the drainpipe, past the entrance and the water and the concrete wall, the otherworldly breeze met us once more. We stared into the depth of the darkness. And then, taking a deep breath, we stepped inside.

We could walk inside the drainpipe as long as we kept our heads down and knees bent. After about ten feet, the light of day faded behind us. We turned on our flashlights and crept forward, spelunkers encountering a corrugated-steel cave. We were followed by the sound of the skateboard's wheels drumming out a steady rhythm against the corrugation.

After what felt like an hour, we stopped and talked briefly, reassuring each other. Outside, the thunderclouds were building in the distance, the winds were picking up. Inside, with the storm out of sight, we felt only the cool breeze flowing through the tunnel. We continued.

Then, on our left, in the glow of a flashlight, we saw another pipe, much smaller and jutting out like a tributary. It opened about halfway up the wall of the main pipe. We would be able to fit as long as we crawled on our hands and knees. There would not be enough room to turn around. We would need to make it to the end, or, if retreat became necessary, we would need to methodically inch backward all the way to the main pipe.

We had not checked the weather report. We had no idea if there might be a thunderstorm that afternoon. The weather was not on our minds. It was darkness, not rain, that scared us.

We deliberated. We ate our cupcakes. Then we followed the tributary to see where it would lead.

· · ·

A PHOTO OF KRIS sits on my bedside table. It was taken by his friend, in front of school on a sunny day, when they were fourteen. Kris wears an oversize navy T-shirt and black jean shorts. His black Colorado Rockies baseball cap is turned backward. On his left wrist a watch. In his left hand, near the bottom of the photo, a closed switchblade. His right elbow rests on his right knee. His right index and middle fingers are extended in a peace sign.

His face is oval, his eyebrows dark and thin as though they were drawn on. His nose is small, his lips thin and pink. He looks like a teenager, like the ones I see on the city bus and think are so young. His skin is smooth and unlined, his facial structure not yet that of a man. Slouching, in his XL shirt, his face looks small. It is simply the camera angle and perspective and the oversize clothes, but his face looks too small for his body, or his body too big for his face.

Kris's expression is hard to read. Relaxed. Intense. Nonchalant. Knowing. Each time I look at it I see something different. If I stare at it for a while, I start to focus on his eyes. His left eye squints ever so slightly more than his right. It is most likely afternoon and he is facing west where the sun is shining. But if I look too long at those eyes, I start to feel uncomfortable. He knows something that I do not.

Looking backward, everything is a sign. Better not to read too much into it; he is just a teenager hanging out on a sunny day like a million other teenagers do and have always done.

The photo has traveled with me across the country several times since college. It sits beside me as I fall asleep each night and is there when I wake up. I do not often look at it closely. It is there, as Kris is, though the details are harder and harder to recognize. On the back, in Mom's handwriting, it says simply:

Kristopher Boelte
6/4/93

5

STILL YOU ARE FADING, falling, drowning out of sight. Photographs collected in boxes and binders. Stories told by Mom and Dad over lunch. Memories holding on by a sliver.

You are in the basement as I am coming home. You are down there now and I am on the bus. You are there alone and I am surrounded by schoolchildren.

It is the last day of classes before winter break. I had a party in homeroom. You had a meeting with Mom and the principal. Then you went home. She returned to work. Now you are in the basement.

I will be the last to get off the bus. Now it is full of excited children eager to begin their vacation. They get off at each stop, one by one. Two by two. They are stepping off the bus. I sit near the back with friends. Felix is driving.

You used to sit in the back too. That is where the older kids sat. You and I would move up to the front seat after everyone else had gotten off the bus. We used to listen to Felix tell stories about Puerto Rico. Then you transferred to another school. You do not hear Felix's stories anymore.

You are in the basement listening to The Offspring and I am on the bus. You are moving boxes around the basement. You are measuring distances. I am laughing at a joke on the bus.

You are down there and I am getting closer. I am hungry. I will find a snack when I get home. Maybe a bowl of cereal from the kitchen. Or I will run downstairs and get a pizza from the freezer in the basement.

What did you eat when you got home? Are you peeling back the plastic wrap from a frozen burrito? Placing it in the microwave. 3:25—You think about a girl you used to know. 3:10—She let you come over to her place. 2:45—Her room was covered with photos of her friends, cheerleading memorabilia, a mirror in which you saw yourself standing there in front of her. 2:10—She slowly took off her clothes. 1:50—She motioned for you to come over to the bed. 1:20—You hesitated, seeing her like that. 0:45—You look up at the microwave. 0:00—You are sixteen years old.

The bus is empty and I am sitting in the front with Felix now. A bandage covers the bridge of his nose. He says that before he drove a bus, he spent years working in the sun. Then he tells me a story about the time he ran with a gang called the Latin Kings. He smiles thinking back on what a reckless teenager he was. His memory appears strong, vivid. He will die years later of cancer. I will hear about it from a friend when I visit Denver in the spring after the ice has melted and everything is green.

I open the front door and call out to you. "Hey, Kris," I say, but you do not answer. I go into the family room and turn on the TV. I sit down and watch *Saved by the Bell.* Then I get up and pour myself a glass of milk in the kitchen. I take a sip and it is cold against my lips. I walk through the house. Around the first floor and then up the stairs. Where are you?

Mom is at work and Dad is at work and you are in the basement. I am upstairs walking from room to room wondering where you are. There are wrapped presents in Mom and Dad's room. They are for you and me. Christmas is just a week away.

Where are you? I am thinking. You are in the basement but already you are a memory fading, photographs in boxes and binders, stories told over lunch.

I sit down in front of the TV, staring, but not really watching, until the phone rings. I get up and walk over to the kitchen. I pick up the receiver and Mom is on the other end and she is talking to me. She asks if you are around and I say I haven't seen you. She is worried. I hear it in her voice. She says there was a meeting at school.

I hang up the phone and sit back down. I stare at the TV for another two hours. I look over at the clock often. I am thirteen and have not yet had a girlfriend or seen a girl without her clothes. The world is out there all around the house and I am in front of the TV. I am here and you are in the basement.

I am thirteen years old. I do not yet know the limits of memory and so have not looked closely at you. I have not etched your image in my mind. I have not recorded your voice to play back later when I no longer know its sound. I am thirteen and I sit in front of the TV with the whole world outside. And you are fading.

Mom comes home and Dad comes home. They are worried and wonder if you might be at a friend's house. Mom makes calls to parents but no one knows where you are. We are there in the house with you but you are not there with us.

Mom asks again if I have looked in all the rooms and I say I have. Then it occurs to me that I have not been downstairs.

Dad is opening the door to the basement. He is walking down the wooden steps one by one. He is bracing himself against the railing as he steps down. I am upstairs with Mom and you are in the basement.

Dad's steps on the stairs are slow and deliberate. He is walking down the stairs. Now he is in the basement. He is screaming now. The world is crumbling in on us. The rafters are being pulled down by your weight.

Mom is dialing 9-1-1. She is talking to the dispatcher. The dispatcher asks if someone can cut you down. It does not matter, though. You have faded.

6

WHITE SAILS DOT THE bay beyond the Golden Gate. It's Saturday, and the water is covered with sailboats. At Point Bonita Lighthouse, on the edge of the Marin Headlands, the wind is constant. Occasionally, a sailboat makes its way out beyond the bridge and into the ocean like a child venturing into the deep end of the pool.

Most of the ships passing the lighthouse are big container ships carrying multicolored cargo boxes bound for Asia. The Port of Oakland, inside the bay, is one of the busiest ports in the United States, and large boats come and go through the Golden Gate regularly.

A group of tourists stands by a railing outside the lighthouse looking out into the Pacific. It's a clear day but they strain to see something. A whale, someone says. He saw it out in the ocean just past the rocks. I look and see only rocks and waves and light.

The view west from the lighthouse is seemingly endless, uninterrupted by rocks or buildings or trees, stretching out for miles toward the horizon, where the container ships disappear into the haze. I stare out in search of the whale whenever someone points—Look!—but I never see it.

Only half of what I see out there is visible. Beneath the waves another world exists out of sight, unknowable from here, where I stand.

Point Bonita's light is visible for eighteen miles on a clear day. The lighthouse was first built three hundred feet above the ocean, in 1855.

At the time, there was a light on Alcatraz Island that could be seen by ships heading straight into the bay, and another at Fort Point, in the Presidio, that marked the south side of the Golden Gate. Point Bonita would mark the northern boundary.

Three hundred feet up was too high, however. When the dense fog was low to the water, ships could not see the light at Point Bonita. The lighthouse was moved lower, to a rock outcropping on the very edge of the point.

Getting down here isn't all that easy. You have to walk a winding path down through the steep coastal hills. Make your way through a small, hand-carved tunnel in the middle of a giant rock. Follow the path as it traverses the rocks on the edge of the ocean. And finally, cross a small suspension bridge that sways with each step, the waves constantly assaulting the rocks below.

I stand near the lighthouse in the bright sun and feel the wind whipping against me. It's the kind of day that the tourists love. The coastline is unbelievably beautiful. Maybe I should just sit down and take in some sun, enjoy the Headlands in its sunny splendor, but I can't help imagining thick fog spread out over Point Bonita.

The tourists around me keep straining to see the whale. I see an old lighthouse keeper finishing his breakfast—fried eggs and sourdough toast—saying good-bye to his wife with a kiss on her cheek, and making his way to his perch in the midst of the fog, walking down the moist path from his residence farther inland, making his way through the dark tunnel carved into the rock. He enters the lighthouse, sets down his lunch, checks on the light, and settles in for another day on the edge of the continent.

He's gone, of course. There's no lighthouse keeper at Point Bonita anymore. Just a national park employee in his brown uniform who's standing in the sun talking to a group of tourists, telling them about the shipwrecks.

More than three hundred ships ran aground in these waters in the years following 1849, during the gold rush. The wrecks continued after Point Bonita was built in 1855. In 1901, the SS *City of Rio de Janeiro* struck a rock near Fort Point in heavy fog. Of the 211 people on board, 131 died. The body of Captain Ward washed ashore near Fort Point two years later, his watch chain still wrapped around his ribs. Wreckage from the ship was still being found in the area twenty years later.

The first lighthouse keepers here used cannons to announce the presence of land when the fog was too thick for ships to see the light. A fog bell—an improvement on the cannon—replaced it, and a steam siren replaced the bell. Now, when fog triggers a laser beam, an electric foghorn sounds twice every thirty seconds. Each foghorn, like each lighthouse light, has a distinctive pattern.

The technology changes, and yet the fog remains difficult to navigate. Ships still use sight and sound, in addition to radar and navigation charts, to find their way. Shipwrecks still happen from time to time.

There is no foghorn today, however. Just sailboats and container ships, sun and never-ending wind.

7

FROM: Kathy Boelte <kathy.boelte@yahoo.com>
TO: Kyle Boelte <kyleboelte@gmail.com>
DATE: Sat, Dec 17, 2011 at 11:06 AM
SUBJECT: dealing with our grief

Dear Kyle,

How are you this year? We find it hard each year from
Kris' birthday, Nov. 6 through at least the anniversary
of his death on Dec. 16. It's not like we don't
think of him other times. At this time of year, each
time frame brings up the questions of what should we
have noticed, what could we have done to prevent his
suicide.

A couple of years ago we bought a frame with about 8
slots for pictures and picked out photos of you and
Kris. We have it in the guest bedroom. Last night we
brought in a box from the garage that has the stuff we
packed up from Kris' bedroom and all the sympathy cards
from friends. We made it through about half the box.

I wish the three of us had worked on grief issues
together. When you went off to college, we hated to say
anything around the anniversary, as you were away from

home and had finals at school at that time. Since then
we've all seemed to have avoided the subject.

You can now go on-line and put in Kristopher Boelte—a
picture of his gravestone comes up. For some reason,
there is even an article in a S. Carolina (or
somewhere) newspaper that picked up the story of his
death. Your essay in Lost magazine comes up either
there or under your name.

Our time in LV may not give us time to talk about Kris
and grief, but if you'd ever like to talk about it,
then or at other times, we would too.

Love,

Mom and Dad

8

A RED-TAILED HAWK FLOATS alone in the clear blue sky. It circles above the quiet neighborhood surrounding Grandview Park, a small hill out in the Sunset District. The hawk searches for prey below. The wind blows strong. Whitecaps crash offshore, beyond Ocean Beach to the west. The hawk sails by and then hovers over the houses, scanning yards for signs of life.

It's sunny, but cold enough at the top of the hill for my ears to hurt. Haze is gathering in the distance. The heart of fog season is still a few weeks off. It starts slowly with fog found in small, unpredictable clusters around the coast. At this time of year, it's hard to know where to find it. Then, at season's peak, fog will surround Grandview Park and everything around it.

To the north, the hawk hovers in the air across from where I stand, riding the wind, its massive wings outstretched. It maintains its position, surveying the ground below. Atop the hill, the ragged hilltop cypress, branchless on the windward side, reach their roots into the ground for support against the wind. I root my feet into the sand while the hawk floats effortlessly overhead.

Grandview is a desert island lost within the city. It rises six hundred and sixty feet above sea level, a perfectly round half circle when seen from Golden Gate Park. It looks green from down below, abundant. But up close, it's mostly sand. The chert, a sedimentary rock, a vestige of an ancient seafloor, is exposed up top. Covering most of the rock, however, is sand, blown here before the hill was cut off from the ocean by houses, roads, and concrete walls.

The plants that grow on Grandview Park are dune dwellers. The Franciscan wallflower. The dune tansy. The bush monkey flower. They live in the sand and must make it through months without rain. No rain, just the cold wind pushing against them. The sand is not being replenished by the wind, not fast enough, anyway. Erosion is a major problem on the hill. Sand falls—is blown, is kicked—down to the streets below, and encroaching development prevents new sand from arriving from the sea.

I stand atop the hill and survey the scene. I'm thirty years old. My childhood memories are fading. The wind tears at the sky. The hawk effortlessly floats above the ground. I'm hunting for remnants of eroding memories. I'm walking around the city in search of fog. I'm trying to figure out what I can see and what is obscured.

9

TWO DAYS AFTER KRIS was found hanging in the basement I asked to spend the night at a friend's house. Was I sure? Mom and Dad asked. Did I really want to so soon? I just wanted to get out of the house. A phone call was made and I was driven over to Rordan's house.

Another friend, Eli, joined us that night. The three of us were good friends, still young enough for sleepovers. We talked into the night, as we always talked when we slept over. The only thing I remember of the conversation, though, is this: "How did he do it?" Rordan asked. "How did he hang himself?"

I did not know the answer. I still don't know the answer, twenty years later. I had not gone down into the basement on December 16, 1994. No one told me how it had been done. I never asked.

Rordan offered a guess that night. Something he had heard. Rumors travel fast. Kris had stood on a stool in the basement. Had used a belt, perhaps. I imagined, then, in my friend's bedroom, my brother hanging in the basement from a leather belt. I immediately tried to forget the image.

The memory of that night fades there, with me trying to forget.

After Kris died, I did not want to go back down into our basement. In fact, I never entered the basement of that house again. I did not want to be alone in that house. I did not want to live in that house anymore.

After school, I would get off the bus early at my friend Shane's house or down the road at Rordan's house. I would stay there with them for a couple of hours until one of my parents got off work and could come pick me up. My friends and I would look through baseball cards. We would do homework. When it was nice out, we would play basketball in the driveway. I sought refuge from our tainted house with friends.

Life continued as it had before, with long conversations about girls and sports and upcoming dances. Life was utterly different.

I came to think that I had grown up, then, in an instant. I continued to sleep over at friends' houses from time to time, to play with baseball cards, to live as a thirteen-year-old boy. But I felt older. That year, many of my friends were going though coming-of-age rites—bar mitzvahs, bat mitzvahs, Afrocentric rites of passage. My close friends were studying and becoming men. I felt much older than them. I felt like I was already a man. Still, I could not sleep alone at home anymore.

Kris's bedroom was at the top of the stairs, on the left. Mine was on the right. A bathroom connected our bedrooms. Down the hall was Mom and Dad's room. The night Kris was found hanging in the basement, I slept on the floor beside my parents' bed. A couple of blankets made up my bed. I slept on the floor beside their bed each night for several months. I slept on the floor and pulled the blanket over my head, every night, until we found a new house nearby, and moved away.

10

WHEN I GET TO the beach, I pull my cap down lower on my head. My jeans are getting wet. My jacket too. There's a light drizzle, a blowing mist, something between rain and wet fog. It changes every few minutes, from rain to mist to nothing at all, just the spray of ocean. The sky is a palette of grays. In front of the gray is the ocean. Blue set against gray. A blue that at once pushes out from and is subsumed by the gray.

The beach is deserted except for the snowy plovers, small shorebirds, which race through the edge of the surf. I walk north up the beach toward nothing in particular, toward a gray nothingness that is no destination at all since I cannot reach it. The snowy plovers run parallel to my path, their legs a blur.

The wind and rain pick up and I head away from the surf to sit under a smooth sandstone cliff. I end up spending most of the afternoon here. The sky and the sea run together. The past and the present push into each other. Colors swirl. The sand is blown around the beach. Everywhere is movement and yet nothing seems to change. I watch the surf break near the beach and listen to the polyphonic ocean. The constant hum. The crashing waves.

The trail back to the car is full of puddles. The smell of spring flowers mixes with the welcoming scent of wet dirt.

The hills in this part of Point Reyes are treeless but green—in spring, anyway—the grass and scrub thick. The seaside sandstone cliffs block the harsh wind. A gentle breeze blows through the valley grass.

On my way back to the car, I occasionally come upon snails making their way across the trail. I stop to watch one as it slowly moves over the dirt and sand. A trail of slime stretches behind it. What is it like to be this snail? What is it like to move so slowly?

I look up at the sky above me. I think about the band The Offspring. One moment I'm thinking about the snail and the next I'm thinking about The Offspring. I'm not sure why. I remind myself to look up the band when I get home. Kris was listening to them on that last December day.

I've driven out to Point Reyes today to see the fog. It's one of the foggiest places in the world. There isn't any fog here today. Light rain and snails, but no proper fog.

The Offspring. The song "Come Out and Play." The black-and-white video that was playing on MTV all summer.

I look down at the snail in front of me. I watch it gliding across the trail on its slime. How does it experience this drizzle? What does it think of the missing fog?

The snail's world is the world in front of it, underneath it. Individual pebbles sit idle along its path like cars dotting a busy commercial street. The grass rises high above it like the towers of the Financial District. Not that it can actually see any of this all that well.

A snail sees light and dark shapes from eyes on its tentacles. Its eyes are primitive. This snail cannot see me clearly, but from a distance it may sense something dark above it.

It continues on across the trail. Not once do I see it stop to look out at the view.

A snail can feel the ground vibrating, can sense something moving near it. Does this one sense me here above it, watching it, breathing in the salty sea air? It may have some sense that I am here, I suppose. It probably doesn't care. It has no brain to speak of—just bundles of nerve cells throughout its body. Ganglia for the senses, for the mouth, for the foot. It smells food. It can remember the smell of something it ate months ago and seek the smell later when it's looking for food.

Snails don't do well in dry conditions—they either die, or they sleep. Snails' relatives—abalone, clams, oysters, and most of the other eighty-five thousand species of mollusks—live in the ocean, while snails do their best to keep moist on land.

A snail can sleep for days or weeks or months or years: aestivation, in heat or dryness; hibernation, in the cold.

A living snail was once glued inside a glass display at the British Museum. It was thought to be dead but was actually just sleeping. When museum employees discovered it was alive they released it. What did the snail remember of its trip to the museum? The exhibits and people, the lives of those walking by? Nothing, I bet.

11

SUBURBAN DENVER SCHOOL TRYING TO HALT THE RISE IN LSD USE

By MOLLY HALL
The Associated Press

HIGHLANDS RANCH, Colo.— One student is dead, another is recovering from an overdose, and at least 17 are being punished for the spread of LSD in this wealthy Denver suburb.

"What we're learning is that in the Denver metro area, there's been an influx of LSD," Principal Jim Wallendorf said Tuesday. "It's weak, like a $2 hit is like having a beer or two."

The investigation began three weeks ago because of rumors around Highlands Ranch High School that LSD use was on the rise, Wallendorf said.

The probe was about a week old when a 14-year-old student had a severe reaction to mixing his prescription medication with LSD. After that, frightened students began coming forward and telling investigators about dealers selling to younger students, he said.

"From that we were able to make a break in the case and say, 'Where did you get it?' ... and talk about the seriousness of the issue," Wallendorf said.

Their tips led to 14 students being suspended, and three others facing expulsion hearings. Criminal charges were being prepared against two other students suspected of dealing large amounts of drugs. One of those students — 16-year-old Kristopher Boelte — killed himself last Friday, said Sgt. Attila Denes of the Douglas County Sheriff's Department.

Police would not say how he died, or how much LSD he and the other student are suspected of selling.

Denes said that "while (the investigation) may not have directly precipitated the suicide, it may have had something to do with it." The other student, who has been expelled, may still face criminal charges, he said. There have been no arrests.

Denes said the students are dealing or using "dirty LSD," which was mixed with amphetamines or other drugs and more likely to have bad side effects.

The suspended students all received the maximum five-day penalty for alleged use of illegal substances, the school district said. The students facing expulsion are suspected of distributing drugs, which also included marijuana.

Wallendorf said the rise in drug use may be linked to the increase in the school's enrollment — from 1,500 to 1,800 since last May. That rapid growth may make some students feel alienated and turn to drugs, he said.

"It's so crowded now that really we don't know the kids the way we did before," he said.

12

Puzzled, Julia asked why I don't care about my birthday. She's a birthday person. Two months after we met, we traveled to Vancouver Island, in British Columbia, for her birthday. We stayed at a place she had seen in a magazine several years earlier.

We met in late July, just a few weeks after my birthday. I was sitting on a barstool by the door inside a small jazz club in the Haight. Out of the foggy summer night Julia walked in, petite with rosy cheeks and a questioning smile. We saw each other as soon as she walked through the door. I stood and approached her. We ordered bourbon. That's how it started.

Julia asked how I celebrated my birthday that year and I said I didn't do anything in particular. I haven't paid much attention to dates in years. I can't remember the last time dates mattered much to me. Christmas, as a child I guess. Or my birthday, as a child.

Later, our glasses empty, we walked out of the bar together, into the billowing fog.

. . .

An email from Mom showed up in my inbox last December.

How are you this year? We find it hard each year from Kris' birthday, Nov. 6 through at least the anniversary of his death on Dec. 16. It's not like we don't think

of him other times. At this time of year, each time
frame brings up the questions of what should we have
noticed, what could we have done to prevent his suicide.

What did I know? What could I have done? There is a reason, no
doubt, these memories are so hard to recall. I used to think I thought
of Kris everyday. Sometimes I think I must still.

I replied to Mom's email and told her I think about Kris often. The
grief is usually associated with stories or books or movies, I said, not
dates. Sometimes it comes out of nowhere, when I'm walking down
an empty beach, when I'm watching a movie, when I'm listening to a
friend talk about something unrelated. He remains a big part of my
life, I told her, though his death has become less of a struggle than it
once was, his life more simply a part of who I am.

I did not mention how much I have forgotten. I did not mention
how I feel when I am home alone at night.

When Julia and I were first dating, we were driving in the city on
a sunny day and "Come Out and Play" came on the radio. I reached
over from the passenger seat and changed the station. I did not explain
why, and she changed it back.

"It's a good song," she said.

"It has too much significance," I replied.

Months later, we started watching *Better Off Dead*. An eighties
classic, Julia had told me. We did not finish it.

In middle school and high school, everyone knew my *situation*. It
was a small school. My friends were adept at steering a conversation
away from trouble. In college, I had to tell people about my brother's
death for the first time. I had to choose who would know. I changed
the radio from The Offspring on my own. As an adult, meeting new
people has always meant deciding who to let in. My circle is small.

When I read Mom's email in December, I did not look up Kris's
name online. I looked out the window at the rain falling from the sky
and thought about my parents' pain—the loss of a child—a pain I

cannot comprehend though I share in it. The rain fell off and on all night.

. . .

ON OUR SECOND DATE, Julia asked about my family. We were in a dimly lit Italian restaurant on Valencia Street. It was a situation I had faced many times before. Explain the unpleasant details of our family's particular struggle, or brush it off until some later date. I looked across the small table at Julia and began telling her about Kris. About our family, Kris's life, his death, what followed.

I had just come back from a backpacking trip in Colorado with two close friends, I told Julia. As we hiked up a twelve-thousand-foot mountain, surrounded on all sides by peaks jutting up into the sky, I collapsed to the ground in tears.

We had been hiking through a trail-less canyon, crossing over and over again through a swift, winding creek, the water rising above our knees, as we made our way deeper into the wilderness. We found a trail and headed up Oh-Be-Joyful Mountain.

The three of us have been friends for twenty years. They knew Kris, lived through his death, the memorial service, the slightly slanted world that followed. Hiking up the mountain, we talked about friendship. What it means and what it requires. Out of nowhere it hit me, like a chef's cleaver striking bone. I had been keeping new people at a distance, afraid of allowing them into my life, afraid that I might lose them.

I collapsed to the ground in the middle of the trail, I told Julia, as the restaurant blurred around us.

. . .

Months later, I remember and reread Mom's email. I then type *Kristopher Boelte* into a search engine. Somehow it has not occurred to me to do this, in the decade or more in which the Internet has been a part of daily life. I click on the first result and see Kris's gravestone. I wonder what kind of business this is. Who walks around the country's cemeteries taking photos of gravestones? Who enters the keywords so that we can find them? Who chooses to run ads on such a site?

I return to the search results and, near the bottom of the first page, find the AP article. It is a scanned copy of page 6A of the *Savannah Morning News* from December 21, 1994. "Suburban Denver school trying to halt the rise in LSD use" sits above Christmas ads for perfume, and silverware, and Rolexes—"There's nothing like the gift of an elegant Rolex time-piece to tell that special someone how you feel."

I forget, for a moment, that my mom had mentioned the article in her email. I forget about dates, and birthdays, and movies. I reread the article a second and third and fourth time. I start to remember.

13

On April 8, 1994, The Offspring, a punk band from Huntington Beach, California, released their third album, *Smash*. It was an inauspicious day to release a rock album. Kurt Cobain's body was found the same day at his home in Seattle. A shotgun and a suicide note were found nearby. "I haven't felt the excitement of listening to as well as creating music, along with really writing . . . for too many years now," it read, in part. The twenty-seven-year-old Cobain had shot himself in the head several days earlier.

When *Smash* came out, The Offspring's front man, Dexter Holland, was on a leave of absence from his molecular biology PhD program. As a teenager, he'd been the valedictorian of Pacifica High School, and had met bandmate Greg Kriesel on the cross-country team. A bright and "normal" guy in a music world full of troubled souls, Holland was in grad school because no one really made money in punk—The Offspring's previous album had sold fifteen thousand copies. Though their songs were dark and dealt with teenage alienation, violence, and low self-esteem, the band was mostly just messing around and having fun. It was a side project. Then "Come Out and Play" was released.

Holland was sick at home on the couch watching *Montel Williams* when he came up with the idea for "Come Out and Play." The show was about kids who needed to bring guns to school for protection. *God, that's so ridiculous*, he thought as he watched. But he also thought it'd make for a good song.

Whether they identified with the gang members, or were playing out early-nineties gangster fantasies via punk rather than rap, or were

in on the joke, or if they even heard all the lyrics over the hypnotizing rhythm and Middle Eastern guitar riff, suburban kids across the
country ate it up.

You gotta keep 'em separated

Like the latest fashion
Like a spreading disease
The kids are strappin' on their way to the classroom
Getting weapons with the greatest of ease
The gangs stake out their own campus locale
And if they catch you slippin', then it's all over, pal
If one guy's colors and the other's don't mix,
They're gonna bash it up, bash it up, bash it up, bash it up

Hey, man, you talkin' back to me?
Take him out
You gotta keep 'em separated
Hey, man, you disrespecting me?
Take him out
You gotta keep 'em separated
Hey, they don't pay no mind
If you're under eighteen, you won't be doing any time
Hey, come out and play

The single was released in March. That summer, a mostly black-
and-white music video featuring the band playing in a garage, dogs
fighting for a toy, and shots of snakes and snake charmers was all over
MTV. The song reached No. 1 on the Billboard Modern Rock Tracks
chart. The album sold more than eleven million copies and became
the best-selling independent-label album of all time. Holland didn't
need to return to school.

By the time you hear the siren
It's already too late
One goes to the morgue and the other to jail
One guy's wasted and the other's a waste
It goes down the same as the thousands before
No one's getting smarter
No one's learning the score
Your never-ending spree of death and violence and hate
Is gonna tie your own rope, tie your own rope, tie your own

Hey, man, you disrespecting me?
Take him out
You gotta keep 'em separated
Hey, man, you talkin' back to me?
Take him out
You gotta keep 'em separated
Hey, they don't pay no mind
If you're under eighteen, you won't be doing any time
Hey, come out and play

14

THE SUN IS RISING in the east over the Berkeley Hills. The sky that surrounds it is a calm clear blue. The bay is placid in the still morning air. I'm walking up a concrete drainage ditch behind warehouses that butt up against the base of San Bruno Mountain, south of San Francisco. Concrete and steel warehouses on one side, scrub and tall grass on the other.

Above me, a bank of fog blowing in from the west meets the mountain. Wisps of fog linger near the peak but cannot make it past. Instead, the fog splits, flowing to the north and south of the mountain, finding its way along the valleys on either side.

I want to be enveloped by this fog. I want to see the world obscured and then see it come back into view. I want simply to close my eyes and feel the world wet on my skin. Stand for a moment inside the fog, breathe it in, and feel it in my lungs. I want to live inside this wisp of white, if only for a moment.

The fog won't last long. The sun will beat it back soon.

A trickle of water flows at my feet. I walk slowly, awkwardly, one foot on each side of the V-shaped concrete ditch. I pass over a few empty bottles, a small bag that once held potato chips, a hamburger wrapper. On the other side of a chain-link fence, a truck driver sits in his cab waiting to unload his delivery when the workday begins. Small birds dart through the air in front of me. I hear them chirping all around. They don't seem to notice the difference between the man-made and the natural. They fly from concrete to scrub and back again.

After ten minutes of precarious walking, I reach the end of the ditch. A steep canyon rises up in front of me. There is no trail. Thick scrub is everywhere. I head up into it, attempting to push branches out of the way, but they won't budge. I try to step through the mess and up the slope, but it's too steep. I look up to the peak above and the fog rolling in, then down at the scrub in front of me. I look for a way forward, a break in the thick vegetation, but I cannot find one. Not without bushwhacking, and I don't have a machete. I retreat. There must be another way up.

As I'm driving away from the warehouses, I see an old fire road that climbs the northeast ridge. I pull over to the side of the road and look up at the fog on top of the mountain. I start walking up the dirt road, hoping I've found a way to the fog. After about a quarter mile, the road narrows to a footpath that climbs straight up the ridgeline.

The sun has moved higher into the sky. I take off my jacket and walk in jeans and a T-shirt. The fog continues to flow on either side of the mountain. Continues to gather at the top. I'm walking on the edge of the fog line. Like Twin Peaks, San Bruno Mountain is a barrier that the fog cannot penetrate. Only when it has built into a great mass along the coast will it overtake the peaks. For now, it settles into the Coast Range's small valleys.

As I approach the top of this little ridge, I begin to hear the sounds of heavy machinery. I reach the top of a false summit and peer down the ridgeline below. Earthmovers scrape the ground, reinventing the topography, making way for a few more houses on the edge of the park. I mutter under my breath. To get to the fog, I'd need to walk down this ridge—one hundred feet of elevation is all—then back up as it rises once more. The construction is in my way. I'm blocked once more. I look up again and see the fog hanging on, lingering on the top of the mountain above me, just out of reach.

. . .

MEMORIES OF KRIS OFTEN come without warning, on their own, triggered without intention. In the middle of a run. When a song comes on the radio. Upon waking, still half asleep. I sometimes come in exhausted and sweaty after a long run and head straight for a pen and paper. I write down a few sentences before I forget whatever it is I just remembered.

Trying to remember is often a good way not to remember.

. . .

I TRY THE NORTH ridge, starting from a quiet neighborhood tucked into the hill. People are beginning to leave their houses, climb into their cars, and head to work. I walk up a sandy path, beside a grove of young eucalyptus, past a few more houses, and then onto a small dirt road. I climb higher, knowing that I've taken too long. I've let the sun rise too far. I'm still not even close to the top and the sun is beating down on me.

Fatigued, I reach a plateau. The sky is bright blue. The path I'm walking on comes to a dead end at a chain-link fence. I look to the southwest and see the Santa Cruz Mountains, a spine leading to Silicon Valley. To the west is the ocean, blue to the edge of the earth. The sun continues to rise. San Bruno Mountain is directly south of me. The fog has burned off. The sun is too much for it today. It will return tonight, continue to flow around this mountain through the gaps. In a few days it might be strong enough to overtake the whole city. For now, I'm left standing by the chain-link fence, grasping for something that no longer exists.

15

Fade into backyard patio.

"Hey Dad. Hey Dad didja know what?" Kris says as he climbs over a toy truck. "Whhooa," he lets out, as he stumbles over the truck, falling.

"Daddy don't picture yet," he says, standing back up.

"No picture yet?" Dad replies from behind the camera.

"No." He shakes his head and stands up. "No no don't picture yet. Daddy don't picture yet Daddy. Daddy Daddy don't picture yet," Kris says as he wanders around the patio.

"Kris, can you sing happy birthday to Kyle?" Mom asks as she carries me outside and settles me in a high chair. A few presents balance on the table.

"Kyle, happy birthday to you," Kris sings. "Heyyyy! Heyyyy! Kyyyle. You got a pretty neat present. Don't you want this one?"

"Can I unwrap this for Kyle?" he asks Dad.

"Mm-hmm," says Dad from behind the camera.

"Ok," Kris says, and starts unwrapping. He glances up and sees Mom. "Mom, can I unwrap this for him?"

"You know what, Kristopher? This one's for you and that one's for Kyle," Mom says, handing Kris his present. "Why don't we let Kyle open it. This one's for you. A present for you on Kyle's birthday."

"Can I have it! Let me see what I got. My present!"

Mom brings a birthday cake outside and places it in front of me on the table. She lights one candle.

. . .

THERE IS AN HOUR of footage on our old family video. Mom and Dad took it to a shop in a strip mall several years ago to be copied over from VHS to DVD. They gave me a copy that I watch from time to time. Some of it is filmed in an unintentionally abstract style. Extended shots of ceilings, grass blowing in the wind, and blank walls, as voices speak from out of view. They filmed Christmases and Halloweens and birthdays, even a few ordinary days when we were young.

. . .

KRIS IS STANDING ON the sidewalk in front of the house in Satanta, Kansas, in boots, jeans, winter coat, a red-and-white winter hat. Snow is on the ground. He walks into the front yard. He walks in circles, around and around, watching as his feet leave their marks. He stands in front of the camera, quietly, looking straight into it. The wind blows into the microphone.

I am in the front of the house in Sublette, Kansas, holding a hose. I am watering a bush. Kris comes over. I chase him with the water. We scream with laugher and run around the yard. Water is everywhere. The hose stretches. It will not go any farther.

16

Julia and I are sitting at the table having dinner when the light outside begins to change. Spring is far enough along that dusk is still an hour or two away. But the light outside the window has softened, as if dusk had arrived two hours early today. We keep eating. Then suddenly I remember—we had discussed it earlier in the day and then forgotten—that there is a partial solar eclipse tonight. We leave our unfinished plates on the table and head outside.

The sky is mostly clear. Julia takes out a piece of paper with a pinhole in it. She holds it up to the sky and we turn our backs to the sun to see the crescent shadow fall on the ground in front of us. Across the street, the eclipse is alive in the shadows of the tree leaves on the houses. A thousand crescent eyes flickering.

We walk up the street toward Bernal Hill where our neighbors are milling about. Like a child, I want to look up at the sun. I want to see the eclipse with my naked eyes. To experience it directly, rather than its shadow cast on the wall, the ground. I do not look up at it. We keep walking.

The hill is crowded with young people in wool sweaters and down jackets, all here to watch something they cannot in truth see. They mill about the hill looking at shadows. Some hold telescopes, or tubes of cardboard, or other homemade viewing devices. All hoping to catch a glimpse.

We look like a flock of pilgrims or religious devotees congregating on the hilltops. All except a group of teenagers smoking cigarettes behind a fence at the top of the hill, behind posted keep out signs, who ignore the sun altogether.

I take Julia's hand in mine as we trace the contours of the hilltop. We watch the eclipse as best we can. And in this moment—a moment like a million other moments already passed, already written about, already celebrated—we see the world as it is anew.

The light is so soft, a faded yellow. The temperature is dropping. The sun is not completely blocked, though it is close—85 or 90 percent. To the east, the bay's waters are muted blue. To the west, the fog builds over the Sunset District. The weather forecast calls for clear, fogless skies, but as we stand on the hill, not-watching the sun in the sky, the fog grows stronger.

San Francisco Bay was discovered by Europeans not from sea but rather from land. For two centuries, ships sailed up and down the California coast past Point Bonita without seeing the strait to the east that connected the interior bay to the sea.

In June 1579, Francis Drake sailed by it before anchoring in a smaller horseshoe-shaped bay to the north. Drake, like many other explorers and merchants after him, probably missed the strait due to the sea of fog that often covered it. He claimed the land, in what is now Point Reyes, for Queen Elizabeth, attempting to take control of—to his mind—unexplored wilderness. He left a brass plate nailed to a post.

BEE IT KNOWN UNTO ALL MEN BY THESE PRESENTS

June 17, 1579

By the Grace of God and in the Name of Herr Majesty Queen Elizabeth of England and Herr Successors Forever I Take Possession of This Kingdome Whose King and People Freely Resigne Their Right and Title in the Whole Land unto Herr Majesties Keepeing. Now Named by Me an to Bee Knowne unto All Men as Nova Albion.

G. Francis Drake

A brass plate turned up in 1936 on the shores of the San Francisco Bay on the other side of the Coast Range. Some claimed it as evidence that Drake had actually discovered San Francisco Bay. Others thought the plate had been picked up by someone in Point Reyes and left near the larger bay. (In 1977, thorough testing demonstrated that the plate was a fake.) Today, Drake's Nova Albion is simply known as Drakes Bay.

I first read this account in Harold Gilliam's *San Francisco Bay*. I found an old hardcover copy in a small bookstore in Point Reyes Station one drizzly day. The book had belonged to a dentist from Novato, on the other side of Marin County. He stamped his name and address into it like a later-day Drake and had written the date—*November 4, 1957*—in the gutter, in blue ink. I found it in a provincial stack of books in a corner, a consolation prize on a day stingy with fog.

In October of 1769, Captain Gaspar de Portolá led a small party of Spaniards on an overland expedition, setting out from San Diego with hopes of reaching Monterey Bay, which Europeans had first explored in 1542. Portolá overshot Monterey and ended up in the mountains above Half Moon Bay. It was October and the sky was clear. Portolá could see the Farallon Islands in the Pacific and Point Reyes to the north. He realized his mistake and decided to turn back south. The party was in need of food, though, so he sent out scouts to hunt game before decamping. They came back with news that they had seen a vast inland lake. Portolá didn't seem to care.

"Portolá was not impressed by the discovery of the new bay, neglecting even to give it a name," writes Gilliam. The fog had hidden the bay from sailors for two hundred years. When Portolá found it, it wasn't what he was looking for, so he didn't see it for what it was and moved on. "He was concerned with the fact that the way to Point Reyes was not open," Gilliam notes, "and even more concerned that the hunters had been unsuccessful bringing back a good supply of meat."

. . .

JULIA AND I BEGIN walking down the ridge toward our house. Lights across the city are starting to come on. It will get lighter before it gets dark, but darkness is around the corner.

The fog is making its way out of the Sunset, toward Bernal Hill. The eclipse has summoned it, conjured it, brought it to life in the Outside Lands. It swirls and tumbles and breathes its moist breath on the back of our necks.

This partial eclipse is almost complete. San Francisco will not see a total solar eclipse until December 31, 2252. I look out at the city below us and cannot imagine what that will look like. Forget the darkness. I cannot imagine what the world, what San Francisco, will look like on that date. The past is hard enough to remember. The present hard enough to describe. The future, this place, these hills and valleys, these houses and people, this coast, what will it look like in 240 years?

Dinner is waiting on the table where we left it.

17

WHEN I WAS A teenager, it occurred to me that it might be possible to film all of one's life. Nothing would need to be lost to memory's failings. There would be no gaps. No missing sections. No intermission. No need to remember, even, just the ability to watch.

I was just beginning to forget then. One day I looked up and realized I no longer knew what Kris's voice sounded like. I had been holding on to it like a photograph in a pocket close to the chest. But it gradually slipped. And then one day it was gone.

I forgot the voice but never forgot the day I lost it. Standing in a high school hallway, I told Shane that I could no longer remember Kris's voice. I lamented the loss, as if by losing the memory of the voice I had somehow lost a living part of Kris. I was sixteen when I lost it, the age Kris was when he silenced himself at the end of the noose.

Videoing one's life was unworkable, I decided. To watch everything would require a second lifetime. The more I watched the video, the more video there would be of me watching video. Would I want to watch myself watch myself living ad infinitum? The whole idea was absurd. It was a scheme to capture potentially lost memories, but at the expense of living. Living requires some forgetting. Our bargain with time.

· · ·

I DO NOT REMEMBER much of middle school. I realize this while talking to Shane and Julia. We are sitting in our living room on a clear spring day. I wouldn't think twice about my own memories of those years if Shane's and Julia's memories of the same time in their lives were not so clear, as if the actions they describe happened just last week.

I remember the general outlines, the stories that we continued to tell about middle school into high school. I remember getting ready for dances at Shane's house. Combing our hair in front of a mirror and talking about who we would dance with. The expectant excitement of it. I remember a basketball tournament Shane and I played in. How we lost the last game of the tournament. A tragedy in our minds at the time. I remember teachers, and where their classrooms were situated in the school building just as I remember the layout of the two houses our family lived in in Highlands Ranch. The geography of memory.

I recount to Shane and Julia a story about another kid getting in trouble for jumping out a second-story window at school, just for the fun of it. It was reckless but he wasn't hurt; the window wasn't that high. I remember the day it happened, I tell them. The brick two-story building. The kid's name, even.

You weren't actually there, though, Shane reminds me, with a smile of recognition. It was just something we talked about in high school. The kid had transferred to another school by then, but the story was something of a minor legend. Or the kid was a legend, not the jumping. The story just one small part of his fame.

I allow myself a little smile as I shake my head. Some of my memories are not even my own.

Shane and Julia have countless stories from middle school. They know dates and names and details. And as Shane tells stories from our childhood, they became real to me. Memories open up, unfold. The memories are there, I start to think, most of them, tucked away, obscured but accessible, hidden in crevices of my mind. As a memory emerges, others come too.

How we played football in Eli's backyard. The open gate that marked midfield. Going inside afterward for lunch—always peanut butter and jelly on homemade bread cut into quarters, served with chips and salsa.

How Shane and I went to see the band Live at Red Rocks with my uncle in eighth grade—our first real concert. The acoustic set they played halfway though the show; the old couches the roadies had brought out for the band members to sit on while they strummed their guitars.

How shy we were to talk to girls when we went to an amusement park. Working up the courage to introduce ourselves, to say something to them.

Playing basketball at the end of the day at the health club we worked at as camp counselors in the summer. How much we looked up to the older counselors, high school and college students who drove Jeeps and convertibles who were as cool as cool could be.

Walking to the baseball card shop in a local strip mall to look through their piles of cheap cards. Graduating to the record store when we got older. Flipping through bins of CDs in their plastic cases.

A cascade of memories comes to me as Shane speaks, one after another, snapshots rather than film, the prosaic details intact.

18

I HEAD UP A dirt path in the Presidio, in the northwest corner of the city, passing a few stray sand dunes as I walk, remnants of the city's former wild self. Small yellow and purple flowers have popped up through the sand. A third of San Francisco was sand dunes, but the city's steel and concrete now covers most of the dunes. I walk north past the dunes, amid the Monterey cypress and chirping of birds. The sound of the highway behind me retreats as I get further into the forest.

No forest walk in this city can last long, and just like that I exit the trees at Immigrant Point, on the edge of the continent, high above the Pacific Ocean. In the clear distance, I see Point Bonita Lighthouse in the Marin Headlands, across the water. Behind the lighthouse, miles farther, Point Reyes juts out into the Pacific. These places are becoming markers for me, signifiers of what, I'm not sure.

I walk the Coastal Trail, tracing a ridge of serpentine cliffs. I round a sweeping bend. All at once the Golden Gate Bridge appears, rising up above the water in front of me. Its suspension cables gracefully curve like the crests and troughs of a set of waves. In counterpoint, the deck forms one long, almost imperceptible arch. Magnificently orange, the bridge sits against the blue of the sky and water. I watch a giant container ship leave the bay from under the bridge, slowly plying westward toward Asia. I keep walking.

I come upon Battery Boutelle, a concrete artillery battery built in 1900 to defend San Francisco from seaborne attack. I climb up a set of stairs and then another. I'm on top of the battery now, where a slightly slanted concrete platform one hundred feet across faces the Pacific. A great fog bank is forming miles away over open ocean. Here it is still sunny, though the wind blows constantly. I put on a jacket.

I'm not sure chasing the fog makes any sense. What do I hope to accomplish? Besides, I've tried chasing after it, and chasing doesn't seem to work.

I sit down on the concrete, warm to the touch from the afternoon sun. I decide to stay in one spot for a while. I want to see what happens if I just pay attention. Watch the wind blow through the tall grass on the edge of the cliffs. Feel the sun on my face. The warmth of the concrete beneath me. I close my eyes and listen to the wind as it meets the land.

I hear the cars on the bridge in the distance, a strong river behind a bend. I open my eyes and look over toward the bridge. For a time— five minutes, an hour, I'm not sure—I watch the traffic endlessly flowing in both directions. I watch the water flow out of the Gate into the Pacific. I watch the crowds of tourists from across the world walk the edge of the bridge's deck, stopping occasionally to peer over the short railing into the depths below.

And when I finally look up, I'm caught off guard by a cloud forming above me. Where did it come from? I lie down on the warm concrete and stare up at the sky. The sound of the traffic fades away as I watch the cloud. It blows inland and yet appears to stay where it is. I watch it coming into being again and again. Out of blue sky the wisps of white stratus appear. I look for the moment, the precise moment, when the cloud begins. I cannot catch it. Just blue sky. Then white wisp.

When does a memory become a memory?

I glance back at the horizon and see the container ship slowly making its way west. My thoughts drift in and out as the fog builds and the ship sails further into the horizon. Memories come and go and I make no effort to hold on to them. The sky and my memories merge somehow, and I tremble as if the earth is shaking. I lie there and breathe in the cool salty air and watch, transfixed, as the fog flows overhead.

Perhaps another hour passes. The fog continues to flow inland, but the point at which it originates moves farther and farther out over the ocean. In the background, a fog bank appears over Tennessee Valley in the Headlands. And another over Lands End to the southwest. The land on either side of my vision becomes obscured. I sit up and turn around. A solid mass of gray looms behind me. I am becoming surrounded.

I turn back to the ocean where the fog is being born in front of me. The container ship has long since disappeared into it. The fog continues to grow stronger. Darker now. Thicker. I am alone within the fog.

There is a place inside where the fog builds, beautiful and unknown and looming. We sometimes come across it by accident, alive with aftershocks of feeling.

The fog bank in front of me is about to swallow up the world. It pushes to the east, the tops of the bridge disappearing. It's a mass of gray. A shadow forming over everything. The wind continues to blow cold. I stand and welcome it—all of it—the wind and the fog and my small part in it. I breathe it all in. The fog moves ever lower over the bridge, until it hovers just above the deck, and holds there into the night.

19

WHEN WE WERE YOUNG, Kris and I would wake up early on Christmas morning and tiptoe downstairs to see what was under the tree. It was a grand sight. The living room was always full of wrapped boxes. We would quietly walk around the room, picking up packages, shaking them to see if we could guess what was inside, checking the cards to see who they were for.

Then we would go upstairs and get Mom and Dad. When we were really young, we would wake them as soon as we were up, but as we got older we would wait until at least seven. They would get dressed and come downstairs and put on coffee, and we would all gather in the living room. We started with the stockings, where we would find chocolate and often a small bottle of cologne. We would then take turns opening presents.

I remember the Christmases just as I remember the Christmas scenes from our family movies. They mix together, the memories of what happened and the memories of watching video of what happened. One no more real than the other.

* * *

KRIS AND I, STILL in pajamas, shake out the contents of our stockings onto the living room floor. Dad says, "Christmas, 1984." Kris holds up a brush. He looks over at me. He picks up a small wrapped box and says, "Kyle, there's even a present." I open it.

We move on to the real presents. Kris opens one, a bath towel. "Look what I got, a towel!" he says earnestly. "Ta-da!" He spreads it out and looks at the design. "You wouldn't guess it, but it's a unicorn!"

Kris goes to the corner of the room and finds a small radio. "Look what he brought you, Daddy. He brought a new radio." He carries it toward the camera. "Looks like Santa, he brought us a lot of presents," Kris continues.

Kris sits at a new wooden desk. "How'd he ever get this in?" I sit at a smaller plastic desk, quiet, holding up a piece of paper. "That says *Kyle*," Mom tells me.

Kris opens another present. "Walkie-talkies. Now I can speak!" he exclaims.

"Kyle, we both got these—Kyle, we'll share these." He opens the box. "They're G.I. Joe walkie-talkies! I'll teach you how they work."

"Christmas, 1986."

Kris and I stand in front of the Christmas tree.

"We wish you a merry Christmas, we wish you a merry Christmas, we uh, wish, and a happy new year." We pause for a moment while Kris whispers to me, and then we immediately start in on another song.

"Rudolph the red-nosed reindeer"—Kris puts his hands over his head as antlers—*"had a very shiny"*—he points to his nose—*"nose."* I try to keep up with him. I'm always three words behind.

"Christmas, 1987."

"Yeah, we got up and we didn't want to wake you up," Kris says to Mom. "Then I looked at my watch and it was almost seven o'clock. We got up right on time." Mom asks Kris to check again. He looks at his watch and sees he has read it wrong—it's far earlier than seven. "Ohhh," he says, disappointed, as he brings his hand up to his forehead.

I stand in front of the camera in my new cowboy outfit. "What'd you get for Christmas, Kyle?" Dad asks from behind the camera. "Chaps, and a vest . . ." I speak so quietly I'm barely audible. I list at least five more presents inaudibly before finishing with ". . . a football, and a soccer ball, and a basketball."

"Sounds like you got next year's Christmas this year too," Dad says.

•   •   •

CHRISTMAS IS WHEN WE are reminded of what we do not have. I do not remember Christmas Day, 1994. I cannot recall if we bought a tree before December 16. Certainly we did not buy one after. The presents that were meant for Kris, clothes and CDs mostly, were given to an uncle who came to town for the memorial service. I was given presents. I don't remember any of them.

For a couple of years after Kris's death, we would visit relatives in Kansas City for Christmas. They had kids my age and younger, several of them, and I would play basketball with the oldest in the driveway. We would all pile in cars and drive to their grandparents' house for dinner. On Christmas Eve, we would head to church, a large suburban church to the south of the city near their house. We would wake up Christmas morning and open presents, the group of us. We were like a large family.

For the three of us, Mom and Dad and me, it was a welcome distraction, but it never felt like home. We were with this large family, ten or fifteen people strong, and yet we remained as three.

We have continued to spend most Christmases together. At my parents' house in Colorado. Wherever I was living at the time. Sometimes just the three of us. Sometimes with a girlfriend's family. Now Julia joins us. We still exchange stockings and gifts, a few of them.

Gone is the living room full of presents. Gone is the excitement of Christmas morning. Gone are the songs. Most of all, Kris is gone. His absence is a weight felt more during Christmas than other times of the year. The memories of the Christmases *before*, so good and happy and light, make the present tense a weak substitute.

20

THE PAIN SUBSIDES AS I get out the camp stove. I turn on the gas and hear the liquid drip out, then turn it off again. I light it and a flame rushes forth. It dances above the stove in the wet air. When it dies down, I turn on the gas again and listen to the familiar whisper. I walk over to my bag, dig around, and pull out tonight's dinner: packaged chana masala and basmati rice. I add them to a pot and put it on the stove. The spices come alive, they circle in the air above our campsite. Julia is finishing setting up the tent and arranging the sleeping bags—but that can wait. She follows the smell of the spices back to the stove.

When the food is hot we eat out of the pan. Two spoons. We've been biking all day. Point Reyes is forty miles from San Francisco. The last few miles up Limantour Road, and then again up Sky Trail along Mount Wittenberg, have taken their toll, though the body in motion calms my mind. We eat quickly. The speed does not detract from our pleasure. It's some of the best food we've ever eaten, as camp meals always are. When the pan is empty I walk back to my bag and search for something good to soak up the last of the sauce. Monterey Jack cheese. Chocolate chip cookies. Both work well.

Sated, we look up at the world we've brought ourselves to, too hungry to have seen it before. Live oaks surround us. Douglas firs surround the oaks. Beyond the firs is a great canvas of gray. There is no movement to the fog tonight, no visible movement, just a gray wall. It is wet, very wet, and I reach to pick up my journal before its pages become waterlogged. Droplets of water are already falling from a tall Douglas fir onto the tent.

The world is still, and in the stillness is a quietness, interrupted only by bird songs. Birds surround us, though we can't see them. I hear them to the north, and then to the west. All around us, one at a time. In flocks and then alone again. The thicker the fog gets, the louder they get. The more I notice them, anyway. Then I hear a foghorn in the distance, coming from the lighthouse many miles beyond the gray wall. The birds sing. The foghorn sounds its lone long note. They trade off, the many voices of the birds, the lone voice of the foghorn.

Darkness descends. The fog surrounds me though I can no longer see it. Julia crawls into the tent and I stand outside a little longer, breathing in the moist ocean air. I look around one last time, staring into the darkness.

I crawl into the tent. I kiss Julia, my lips still damp from the sky. We fall asleep next to each other in our sleeping bags, exhausted, listening to it all.

I wake up to the sound of water dripping onto the tent from the trees above. The air is humid; our sleeping bags are damp. The fog has burned off, though, and sun strikes the tent. The wind pulls at the flaps. For a moment I think we've somehow slept in till noon, it's so bright out.

When I unzip the tent and walk outside, I find everything changed. The world has opened up. The gray wall is gone. In its place is the ocean, blue in the distance. Green and blue on blue. A Rothko painting spanning the width of the horizon. The Douglas firs, dark green in the foreground; the ocean, blue against the sky's light blue. On the horizon, amid the haze, I make out the Farallon Islands rising out of the sea.

The wind swirls and I zip up my jacket. A bluebird lands nearby, pauses for a moment, then takes off again. I walk down the trail.

A clearing appears and to the north the land spirals into the ocean around Drakes Bay, where Francis Drake landed more than four hundred years ago. I see Limantour Spit jutting out, a slice of sand surrounded by water. The point is at once impressively solid and delicate. The sand beach of the spit adds yellow to the palette.

A hawk appears above, circling in the sky. I've lost count of the birds I've seen here. I can recognize only a few of the 490 species of birds that have been recorded in Point Reyes. Forty-five percent of all known species in North America are here at some point during the year, in the marshes, and beaches, and forests, and grasslands. Now, without the fog, I see them everywhere. As I walk down the path, they fly out in front of me. I see them but now their songs are diminished, as though sight has robbed sound.

I return to camp to make breakfast. The day will remain clear. We'll hike down Woodward Valley to the coast and find banana slugs as big as our hands. I'll sit in the sun and stare out at the ocean, occasionally watching container ships pass by. I'll read and take a nap. Tomorrow we'll bike home. The sun will stay for a few days.

21

I HAVE TWO MEMORIES from the first day back after winter break.

I was always the first one on the bus, and for the first fifteen minutes there were few other kids on with me. An older kid, one I knew and looked up to, got on near County Line Road and walked through the aisle. Passing, he said, simply, "Sorry about your brother," and continued on to his seat behind me. I erupted in emotion, fighting back tears to keep anyone from noticing.

At school, I sat down in math class—I must have been early because there weren't any other kids there yet—and my math teacher turned from the chalkboard to face me.

"You're a strong kid, Kyle," he said.

I spent the day not-crying.

. . .

MANY METAPHORS HAVE BEEN used to describe memory. The metaphors change with the dominant technologies of the day. "The history of memory is a little like a tour of the depositories of a technology museum," writes Douwe Draaisma, in *Metaphors of Memory*. ". . . Our conceptions of memory are always mixed with the technologies used as metaphors and appear to change completely with each successive image. But after a while, the familiar features show through again, and the similarities are recognized."

Plato wrote of memory as a wax tablet, where impressions are made. "We remember and know anything imprinted, as long as the impression remains in the block; but we forget and do not know anything which is erased or cannot be imprinted," Socrates states in Plato's *Theaetetus*. The metaphorical wax could be of good or poor quality, describing those with strong or weak memories. The impressions on the wax could also be erased and reused, allowing new memories to be stored and old ones to be discarded.

Socrates also suggested that memory is like an aviary, where memories are birds flying about. Later, Augustine wrote of a treasure-house, where like would be stored with like: sounds with sounds, images with images, smells with smells. In the Middle Ages, memory became a library, where one could find old memories stored on shelves. For Cartesians, it was a calculating machine. For Romantics, it was a labyrinth or a giant loom. In the nineteenth century, memory was a switchboard, a phonograph, a camera. In the late twentieth century, memory became the computer, where information could be stored in short-term memory (RAM) and long-term memory (the hard drive).

•　•　•

A STRAY MEMORY FROM high school. Freshman year, my JV soccer coach called me by my last name. "Nice pass, Boelte." "More hustle, Boelte." Though she never called me anything but Boelte, she often called my teammates by their first names. One day at lunch, I was making my way through the salad bar in the cafeteria and I heard a woman say "Kris" in my direction. I glanced up to see my soccer coach looking at me. I looked at her, but she did not say anything else, she just froze.

•　•　•

"WHEN WRITERS ON MEMORY have used their own metaphors, they have quite innocently recorded whatever preoccupied them or surrounded them," Draaisma writes in *Metaphors of Memory*.

"Augustine's imagery for memory describes the fields and caves of Carthage. In Thomas Aquinas's metaphors one senses medieval respect for traditionally sacred texts. . . . Through the centuries metaphors have had a preserving quality and in that way gained an almost museum-like power.

"At the same time, metaphors have given shape to views and interpretations of memory. In a playful metaphor like that of Plato's aviary, the memory does not have the same meaning as in the representation of the memory as the light-sensitive plate of a photographic camera, exposed to the sensory stimuli. One metaphor turns our recollections into fluttering birds which we can only catch at the risk of grabbing the wrong one, the next one reduces memories to static and latent traces. . . . With each new metaphor we place a different filter in front of our perception of memory."

• • •

ANOTHER FROM BEHIND THE fog. A day before Kris's memorial service, the young minister who would give the eulogy talked to me in our living room. He told me a story. About a boy who lost someone close to him. As the adults gathered to grieve, to talk and tell stories, the boy went outside to the driveway. He took his basketball with him. He shot baskets. He did this for hours. For days, he shot baskets.

We all grieve in our own way, the minister told me.

In the days and months and years that followed, I headed outside often. I shot baskets. I ran along footpaths. I didn't say much. I listened to my breath. I listened to my footsteps on the footpath. I looked out in front of me and ran.

22

AGAINST THE QUIET, THE morning draped in fog, I hear only my foot-strike, repeating over and over again. I concentrate on the sound of my feet hitting the pavement. I turn onto JFK Drive in front of the Conservatory of Flowers. A light mist is swirling. The fog is high overhead. Neat rows of flowers are spread out across the lawn—yellows and reds and blues, bright against the gray day. I run west through Golden Gate Park toward the ocean three miles away.

Tall trees surround the road. After I pass the de Young Museum, I turn off onto a dirt path that meanders through the trees. They tower above me, the eucalyptus and Monterey cypress. It's dark here, in the trees. The smell of wet wood rises up from the understory. The trail dives down, and I'm in the Rose Garden. I run at a pace I can hold constant for an hour, a meditative pace, neither too fast nor too slow. I reenter the woods and run along another dirt path before I'm dumped out again onto JFK. I pass a man-made waterfall on my right.

I'm getting warm. Sweat covers my long-sleeve shirt. The cold, damp air meets my skin as I run. Ideal conditions for distance running. There are only a couple of other walkers and runners out this morning on the paved path. When I break off into the trees, I'm alone with the sound of the wind and my feet striking the ground. The meadows I pass, where a few people silently perform tai chi in the early morning, look as though they've been cut out of an ancient forest. I find another dirt path and take it.

The trail continues for half a mile, winding and descending to the ocean. The trees surround me. They shelter the path from the wind.

I look down at the trail in front of me and follow it until it ends at
Ocean Beach.

． ． ．

IN 1868, JUST A couple of years before the park was created, a Santa
Rosa newspaper described the proposed site as a "dreary waste of
shifting sandhills where a blade of grass cannot be raised without four
posts to keep it from blowing away." It was a desert of sand dunes that
stretched to the sea. Frederick Olmsted, the designer of New York's
Central Park, did not think a proper forest park could be created in
San Francisco. "There is not a full-grown tree of beautiful proportions
near San Francisco," he said, "nor have I seen any young trees that
promised fairly, except perhaps, of certain compact, clumpy forms of
evergreens, wholly wanting in grace and cheerfulness."

In 1846, the population of San Francisco was only two hundred. In July 1849, it had reached five thousand. By that December,
thanks to the gold rush, the number was twenty-five thousand. And
in 1870, one hundred forty-nine thousand people lived in San Francisco, mostly to the east of Twin Peaks, though some homesteaders
were to be found in the Outside Lands. These San Franciscans had
the foresight to see the value of nature. They looked around and saw
the loud, crowded, frantic life of the city, and they set aside the park.
"Silence is the universal refuge," Thoreau had written back East. The
park would provide silence and calm within the explosion of human
activity.

In the late 1860s, the land near Ocean Beach was covered with sand
that blew about constantly, sculpting and resculpting a seaside wilderness. Dune-dwelling plants grew in clumps scattered about. On
the east side of the proposed park, the only trees were scrub oak. All
larger trees had been cut down during the gold rush two decades earlier—the entirety of the peninsula south of San Francisco had been

deforested at the time. But on south-facing hillsides, near what is now Stanyan Street, California cherry, lupine, and gooseberry grew.

Golden Gate Park was created on paper by the California legislature in 1870, and over the next 140 years, it was created again and again in the sandy soil of the Outside Lands by designers, gardeners, and workmen. The city was an adopted home to its residents—practically everyone who lived in San Francisco was from somewhere else. They brought with them their vision of what nature should look like. Often, that vision was of the East Coast or Europe, where many of the new inhabitants had been born.

Gardeners scattered a mix of soaked barley and lupine across the dunes to reclaim the land. The barley grew quickly and stabilized the soil enough for the lupine to prosper without being wiped out by the shifting sand. The lupine could survive for up to two years, enough time to get small trees started. From the beginning, the park contained its own nursery. The forest that today, to the casual observer, might look as natural as any other forest, grew up under the care of gardeners. By 1883, more than three hundred thousand trees and shrubs had been planted.

"From the first the plan emphasized that Golden Gate Park was to be natural in appearance—a woodland park," writes Raymond Clary, in *The Making of Golden Gate Park*. "Nothing was to be suggestive of the city. Bridges were to be made of wood and were to be rustic in appearance." When the designers and benefactors of the park looked out over the shifting sands of the Outside Lands, they saw only wilderness. The landscape they found was too wild and unpredictable for their taste. So they created a park that was natural in appearance, a woodland park born out of their imagination, one that was under their control.

. . .

WHEN I REACH OCEAN Beach, I head south. I feel the sting of sand blowing against my face. The ocean stretches out to the west until it reaches the clouds on the horizon.

At Lincoln Way, I turn back into the park and head up to where I started. I'm beginning to feel it, the quiet focus that comes with distance running. I give in to it. The total surrender to movement. I give up control and let my legs guide me. I run up a series of dirt paths through the trees. It's still quiet; the city is just waking up. My mind relaxes. I pass under large tress and through small meadows. I climb steep hills and run up gentle slopes. I let go and just run.

I must have first fallen for the fog on a run like this through Golden Gate Park. Through fog that billowed across the trail as I ran deeper and deeper into it. I've encountered that fog many times running in this park. Alone, with my own movement, as the wet air coats my skin. It's hypnotizing, this feeling. This intense mix of concentration and relaxation.

Am I running from something or running toward something? The question falls to the ground with the scattered leaves, and I move on.

I focus my attention on the path in front of me. I'm getting tired. A pleasant tiredness. The trees around me blur with the fog. My eyes focus on the dirt path in front of me. My mind focuses on the sound of my feet hitting the ground. I focus and relax and lose myself for a moment, the world now a blur and me somewhere within it.

23

"Do you worry your memories are out of balance?" Shane asks me. "Of Kris's death and of his life?"

I pause for a moment. We are on the top of Tank Hill, just north of Twin Peaks. It is a clear day, and we can see the Headlands to the north, Angel Island out in the bay, the Berkeley Hills beyond it. Every neighborhood on the east side of Twin Peaks stands out, for now. I can pick out buildings, and parks, and streets I know. The sun is shining. Clouds are gathering out over the ocean, waiting to move in. Rain will follow.

"The balance is off," I admit. "I've been trying to remember Kris's jokes." I look out at the bay. "He was so funny. So ridiculously funny.

"I've been trying to remember laughing and I can't. I can't remember," I tell him. "I remember being in the house. I remember Dad finding Kris. I remember Kris's memorial service. I remember crying, the tears, but I cannot think of one joke."

I pause and take a breath. I ask what he remembers.

"We all rode the same bus, Felix's bus. Kris would hold court in the very last row, sitting casually with his back to the window," Shane recalls fondly. "We looked up to him. We'd sit farther up, but he would invite us back sometimes, let us into his world. When we went back we would always sit in the seat in front of him, never the same seat or the one next to him. We never stayed for long, but it didn't matter. We were happy to be back there in his presence even for just a couple minutes.

"He'd tell jokes, do impressions, and we'd laugh so hard," Shane tells me. "The jokes would be crude—we usually wouldn't understand them— but we'd laugh anyway because the way he told them was funny. Everyone would listen, would laugh. We felt so special when we were invited back."

I remember once, on the bus, getting into a fight with my friend Michael. He was making fun of my speech impediment. "Say *four fur oranges*," he taunted, though he was smaller than me. I told him if he didn't stop, I'd hit him. I wasn't messing around. I'd count to three and then I'd hit him. I counted. One. Two. Three. He did not stop and so I hit him square in the chest. This is my memory.

On top of Tank Hill, 650 feet above the city, when Shane tells the story, Kris is there. Kris sees Michael making fun of me and he sees me hit Michael. Kris comes forward from the back of the bus and tells Michael not to mess with me.

"He would do that," Shane says, "protect you while letting you fight your own fights."

How do I not remember Kris in this memory? How many memories has he been washed from?

"Kris showed us music. He introduced us to Pink Floyd," he says. "He showed us how you could line up *Dark Side of the Moon* and *The Wizard of Oz*. He explained how you had to be sure to start the music right when the lion roared. How two seemingly unrelated things in the world could come together to make something meaningful."

I have long thought of Pink Floyd as my own, even if I don't listen to the band as much as I once did. A few lines are on Kris's gravestone. I picked them out in the months following his death. I suggested "Hey You" be played at the memorial service. Hearing Shane talk about it now, these choices make more sense. In making them, though, I had taken them on as my own. Though Pink Floyd has always been connected with Kris for me, I had forgotten that Kris had introduced me to the band.

The conversation continues slowly. We pause often.

We look out over the city. Over the bay. Close friends for twenty years now, the two of us. We have spent so many hours over the years talking. We used to wrestle in his basement. Play with baseball cards. Talk into the night at his house. Now we take walks. We remember.

"We were good friends, right?" I ask, as I stare into the distance. "Kris and me?"

"Yeah," he replies, after a long pause. "You were good friends."

24

I'm walking north up the beach near Sloat Boulevard. Couples hold hands as they walk in front of me. A few runners pass me along the edge of the surf. A party is forming. Men carry bundles of wood out to the beach for a bonfire.

I feel the last of the sun's warmth on my face as I look out over the ocean. The breeze is picking up. Clouds are beginning to form around the Golden Gate to the north, hiding it from the container ships sailing into port from Asia. It's been warm and clear today, but the fog is building off Ocean Beach. It's out there now, to the north and to the south. Tonight it will overtake the city. The beach will be empty tomorrow. For now, though, the fog holds off and beachgoers stroll along the water's edge.

The light softens. Blue skies above. The sun orange on the horizon. The waves crash. I keep walking, the sand pushing between my toes. When the sun reaches the horizon, it fades slowly into a bank of fog ten miles off the coast. It sets high in the sky, leaving the beach dimly lit, keeping darkness at bay a little longer.

As I walk Ocean Beach in the dimming light, I think of my friend David, a wilderness guide. He leads groups of young adults on one-, two-, three-month trips into the back of the beyond. The Wind River Range of Wyoming. The red rock canyons of the Escalante. He once spent several rain-soaked months hiking across Patagonia.

When we were sixteen, the two of us went backpacking together in the Weminuche Wilderness, in southwestern Colorado. We drove six hours from Denver to Durango and then boarded a narrow-gauge train to the old mining town of Silverton. Halfway there, the train stopped for us, and we stepped off into an uninhabited mountain valley. We were alone in the wild, where for the next week we would hike through the Chicago Basin, climbing up jagged peaks, eating camp meals, contemplating wilderness and our place in it.

Years later, circumstances conspired so that we were both moving to San Francisco at the same time. David picked me up in Tucson and we caught up as we drove through the desert at dusk. When we got to San Francisco, we rented cheap rooms from an artist and moved our few possessions in. Then we jumped back in the car and drove five hours more to hike the Lost Coast, an undeveloped stretch of rocky coastline in Northern California. We hiked the empty beaches and coastal hills for five days before returning to the city.

We lived in that apartment in the Sunset District—short-term visitors in a flat filled with wild paintings and twenty years of art-project detritus—for half a year before David left once more for Wyoming and the Wind River Range. I stayed in San Francisco to work, to write, to recalibrate my life, still finding my direction after an unexpected breakup a year earlier. I moved to a new apartment when David left, but remained in the Sunset, not yet ready to leave the fog.

In San Francisco, David would wake up most mornings and head to Ocean Beach's unforgiving break, to surf, to be punished by the waves.

"Ocean Beach is true wilderness," he told me one morning after returning from a session. He was at the stove making eggs. I poured milk into a bowl of cereal and sat down at the table. "Out there you are at the mercy of the waves. Control dissipates. Your life is on the line."

Just a few feet from the city of San Francisco lies this vast wilderness. Most beachgoers never see it. They walk across the beach, and the ocean—just a few feet away—is abstract to them. Sound and movement everlasting.

Wilderness, according to the Wilderness Act of 1964, is a desig-
nated area "where man himself is a visitor who does not remain." I've
spent a lot of time in such places. Down long dirt roads and then over
rocky trails. Landscapes where scale is stretched beyond the quotidian.

Wilderness, however, does not simply appear when you cross an official line on a topographic map. It can't be so easily contained. Maybe
wilderness is a place—any place—where the illusion of control slips
away. A local trail in the middle of a moonless night. A rocky ridge
enveloped in fog. The waves crashing against you as you paddle out.

I once ventured out into the Pacific with David on a rented surf-
board of my own. I was tossed about over and over again, fighting for
breath as the waves came crashing down. A set would roll in. I would
push down my board and dive through one wave, gasping for breath
in a fog of foam, only to have it taken from me once again as another
wave came barreling down.

Hours later, we returned to shore exhausted. We dried off, looking
out at the water, at the waves crashing in front of us. I hadn't caught
one wave, not even one, but I felt the draw—being surrounded by
that ocean. I couldn't change it or control it. Chasing after it wouldn't
accomplish anything. I could only observe it, watch it rise and fall, be
present with it, and whenever it came crashing down on me, simply
hope for the best.

Wilderness is like a drug that frees you from the illusion of control.
We head out to these places when we've had too much concrete, too
many cubicles, too many straight lines.

Illicit drugs must be a kind of wilderness, for some, a venturing out
into the unknown.

When I reach Golden Gate Park, the sun is behind the distant fog
bank. Twentysomethings, scattered across the sand, huddle together,
wrapped in blankets. I pause. I watch the fog forming in the distance
over the Golden Gate.

Slowly, the beach empties as night creeps up. I continue walking while the waves crash beside me.

After a while, all signs of the city disappear. For a time, the waves are the only thing I can hear.

Then without warning—or have I seen it for a while from afar?—I suddenly come across a wild bacchanalia. A hundred people circle a bonfire beside the surf, flames ten feet high. A few have broken off and are diving naked into the freezing water, screaming as the water hits them, their forms just recognizable in the darkness. Around the fire the crowd stands with their hands raised into the air. They chant ecstatically, together, a mass of voice. The flames dance and their faces become illuminated.

My path takes me between the frantic crowd circled around the fire and the swimmers plunging into the surf. I silently walk through this wilderness and into the darkness beyond them.

25

Mom & Dad,

   I left for tonight. I've been really messed up by a lot of problems lately. I need time to think. I can take care of myself for at least a night. I'll be back tomorrow after school if you want to call. I just need space to be myself. I can take care of all I need to. Please understand and let me be.

                                                    Later,
                                                    Kris

26

Julia and I fly to western Colorado to visit my parents. They left suburban Denver when I was in college, and now they live beneath the sandstone cliffs of a large mesa near Grand Junction.

At night, we talk of Kris. It is unlike previous conversations I have had with my parents, easier somehow. Years have passed. Julia is here.

I ask Mom and Dad to tell some stories about us as kids. They search their minds and then begin. Anecdotes mostly, beautiful and poignant, they start slowly and then begin to flow. Some are funny, and Julia and I smile as they talk. We age, Kris and I, in the stories, as the night goes on. They speak of birth and death, friends and girlfriends, psychologists and drugs. His baseball cap, his blue hooded sweatshirt, the sheet he brought down to the basement. They talk of what-ifs.

There is a box of Kris's things in my parents' garage. It is clear plastic and contains remnants of his adolescence. Letters and notes and a few baseballs—home-run balls that he had signed and dated. A birth certificate. Adoption papers. Condolence cards. Another box holds stuffed animals and baby blankets. "The happy memories," Mom says.

I ask to see the box, the one with the letters and paperwork. I've never looked inside it.

Mom leaves the room and after a few minutes returns from the garage with the box of Kris's things. She puts it down and begins going through it.

I start to feel uneasy. I say that I'll look through it in the morning. I don't want to see it now. Not tonight. The room has changed now that it is here. Not for Mom or Dad or Julia. They don't seem bothered by its presence. But I feel it as a weight, a weariness.

Maybe she didn't hear me say I'd rather wait till morning. Maybe I didn't actually say it. Either way, Mom takes out a baseball plaque— Most Improved Player. Kris resented the award, she says, because it implied he had not been good to begin with. She hands me the plaque and I hold it, feel its weight in my hands for a moment. Then I put it back in the box.

I say it's getting late. Everyone agrees. We decide it is time to go to bed. We've been talking for hours. I put the lid on the box before leaving the room. I push it down, making sure it's secure.

I have been collecting memories for a while now, but the box is different. It contains physical artifacts. Official documents. Letters from a girlfriend. Notes and school assignments Kris wrote himself. It holds facts and clues to Kris's life, his death. It is more than a box.

Tomorrow I will open the box myself. I will pack up the contents into a small black duffel bag and in a few days we will fly back to San Francisco with it sitting at my feet. When we get home, the duffel bag will sit in the corner of the living room for several days before I open it. I will slowly sift through these artifacts over several months.

Now, lying in bed beside Julia, in the darkness of the night, I think of Kris and the contents of the box. I see Kris though my eyes are closed. The room is hot and I cannot sleep. I just lie there. I do not see Kris as a child, smiling, telling stories, as I'd like to see him. Instead, I see Kris, out in the living room, hanging. I try to think of something else but I can think only of the box, the living room, him hanging. This is what I see until I fall asleep, and with sleep, forget for a while.

. . .

IN THE MORNING MOM and Dad and Julia and I drive out into the desert to look at pictographs and petroglyphs.

The high desert of the Colorado Plateau has its own timescale. After walking through it—the burnt-red sandstone, the pure blue skies, its valleys, the ragged cliffs—we sit in silence and watch the landscape. Millennia of erosion have exposed an untold number of layers. In the silence, with only the sound of the breeze softly blowing, it all seems to stand still. We have to imagine the violent forces of wind and water that have sculpted the rock towers that stand before us. We imagine a great sea. Flash foods. Pressure and force. We carve the valleys in our minds, linking the layers, connecting the visible with what has come before.

Up in the cliffs, beyond the highway and dilapidated roadside motels, strange anthropomorphic figures stare out from sandstone walls into a dry canyon bottom. Buglike, ghostlike, life-size, and drawn in a deep, earthy red, they stand watch over the canyon. Eyeless, legless, hollow eyed, some with antennae, some holding snakes; a sign marks them as barrier canyon petroglyphs (6000 BC–100 BC). Another panel includes small, trapezoidal bodies etched on top of red painted figures and etched mountain sheep: Fremont Indian petroglyphs (600 AD–1250 AD). Another features bison, humans, horses, a shield. They are smaller, painted in white and red: Ute Indian petroglyphs (1300 AD–1880 AD).

We pause in front of each panel, under the hot spring sun, searching for a story, a way to connect the disparate images.

. . .

Kris was very affectionate as a child. We held him in our arms often. He would hug us and give us a kiss on the cheek. When you were born, and we held you more often, Kris was always nearby, ready to show you affection too.

We often read to you both when you were young. One story was about a man who struck out to make his fortune. At a pizza place in town, we ran into one of our clients. Kris had met him just once but remembered his name. He always remembered people's names, even after meeting them just once. When he saw the man, he asked, "George, how is your fortune?"

We told Kris he was adopted early on. We lived in a small town, and everyone knew everything about everyone else. We figured another kid would tell him if we didn't. Plus, we thought he had the right to know. There wasn't a big moment. We talked about it from the beginning.

Once Mom took Kris to a pediatrician in Garden City, a larger town forty miles away. There was an old Model A car out front. Kris asked what it was, and Mom said it was an old-time car. They went upstairs to the waiting room and sat down. A Mennonite family came in—the mother was wearing a long dress and her hair in a bun. "And there's an old-time woman!" Kris exclaimed.

When Mom was pregnant with you, she'd take afternoon naps in our old brass bed. Kris would sit at the end of the bed with his legs wrapped around one of the posts and his hands on the post's flat top. He would steer the bedpost top, asking "Where do you want to go?" He would describe the scenery as he drove the bed around.

Kris visited the hospital right after you were born, when he was three. Afterward, he said he wanted to be from a hospital like you were.

Dad was the county attorney for a while, so he knew all the kids who had gotten in trouble. One kid in particular kept getting in trouble in town. Vandalism, and cruelty to animals, and other serious issues. Dad was worried that Kris was spending too much time with the boy, who lived nearby.

One day he told Kris he thought it would be a good idea if Kris didn't spend his time with the kid.

"Why? Kris asked.

Dad hesitated. He couldn't provide confidential information. Finally, Dad said, "Because I think he may be a bad influence on you."

"But wouldn't I be a good influence on him?" Kris replied.

Another time, Kris got upset at Mom and said, "My real mom is an angel."

We were returning from a vacation, and our short connecting flight from Amarillo was canceled and everyone on the plane rushed to the car rental kiosk. We waited in line, but the man in front of us was the last person to get a car. They had just run out. It turned out that he was going to the same place as we were, and he offered to give us a ride.

Kris, who knew never to get in a car with a stranger, leaned in and asked, "If he's a stranger, why are we going with him?" The man overheard and offered Kris his business card so they would no longer be strangers. Kris took the card from the man, who turned out to be an Archie Cookie rep, and we accepted the ride. We found the business card in Kris's wallet after he died.

Kris came home from one of the first days of kindergarten upset. "What's wrong?" we asked.

"You said I was special," he replied, "but no one at kindergarten knows I'm special."

Once, we all got into an elevator with a heavyset man. Kris asked us out loud if the man was a stranger. We said yes. Kris blurted out that the man was very big. The man looked down at him. "He must be strong," Kris said. The man looked up with delight.

Kris often spoke about being adopted. Once, when we were all getting ready to sit down for dinner, Kris mentioned his birth mother. "Where is that woman?" you demanded, as though she were late to dinner with the rest of the family.

One of Kris's elementary school teachers told us that Kris washed his hands often at school. We saw him organizing and reorganizing his desk drawers often. If we went out and got back late, Kris would cry if he could not take a bath and be clean before bed. We took him to a childhood therapist, who helped him with what they called his obsessive-compulsive behavior. Kris got along with the man really well. The behaviors started to go away, and by the time we moved to Colorado, he didn't need to see the therapist anymore.

Kris's middle school teachers called us in for a meeting. Kris was too funny in class, they said. We suggested they tell him that it wasn't always time to be funny. "The problem is, we can't stop laughing enough to scold him," they replied.

After freshman year, Kris wanted to transfer to another school. We let him do it, but we asked that he see a psychologist to help him with the transition and with the problems he was getting into. Kris saw the psychologist starting in the summer and into the fall, until October. After Kris killed himself, we made an appointment and spoke to the psychologist. He told us that suicide was one of his specialties. He had had no idea that Kris was thinking about killing himself.

Kris once told his preschool teacher that his mom was a skydiver.

In middle school, Kris's Spanish teacher assigned a project to sketch out a family tree and label it with words like grandmother, aunt, *and* uncle. *Kris told us that the teacher had said he could not make a family tree. He was adopted, so he didn't have a family.*

• • •

When he was young Kris was so affectionate. Of course, we've gone back to every day, every event, every time, to try to diagnose when things may have started to go wrong. We start to think about the times when he was not so happy. About what we did.

On December 9, a week before Kris died, the four of us went out to dinner for Dad's birthday. We all had a great time, including Kris. He was really engaged and talked a lot. He had been very moody for several weeks or months, and the change that night was noticeable. It was one of the best nights we had had in a long time. After dinner, Kris suggested that we go for a drive and look at Christmas lights. We thought that was a great idea. When we got to the car, though, he had changed his mind. "No, let's just go home," he said. So we did.

27

A FIELD GUIDE TO SAN FRANCISCO'S FOG

Introduction

"The coldest winter I ever spent was a summer in San Francisco." Everyone in San Francisco knows Mark Twain said that, though in truth he never said it. Nonetheless, every year while much of the country sizzles under the oppressive heat of late summer, San Franciscans look out their windows to find the weather rather winterlike. Those cool summer days come thanks to the fog that forms off the coast and then flows through the city.

In a guidebook, fog is formed by facts. The facts add up, they multiply. Gather all the facts together, and you have an explanation. The mechanics of fog.

I must admit at the beginning that this is no easy task. A lifetime could be spent studying fog and the complex dynamics that bring it to life. "The classification of the constituents of a chaos, nothing less is here essayed." So wrote an old sailor of his attempt to explain the study of whales. Our task is no less daunting.

Fog Defined

Fog, simply put, is visible moisture near the earth's surface. The air often contains invisible moisture, called humidity. Under certain conditions, vapor forms visible water droplets or ice crystals that, when suspended in the air at a high enough concentration, begin to limit visibility beyond them. If visibility is less than one kilometer, then what you see—when you're not seeing what you're looking at—is fog.

The Atmosphere

All over the world, atmospheric pressure is pushing against the earth. The air is pressing down on us. The exact pressure at any given point on the earth's surface depends on local variables, like altitude and temperature. Warm air is less dense than cold air, so its presence causes low pressure; cold air in turn causes high pressure.

Air—when it is dry—cools at about five and a half degrees Fahrenheit for each thousand feet of elevation gain. Hike up a mountain, and it will generally get colder as you get higher. Hike back down, and the air grows warmer.

Nothing stands still—a universal principle. The air flows continuously, equalizing pressure over large areas. Squeeze one end of an inflated balloon, and you are creating a high-pressure area; the air will flow away from the high-pressure area, equalizing the pressure within the balloon. Release the balloon, and the air flows back to where your hands just were, and the pressure is equalized throughout. Similarly, within the earth's atmosphere, air moves horizontally from high to low pressure. This movement of the air is called wind. Wind tends to travel from cooler, higher pressure areas to warmer, lower pressure areas.

Geography

The Bay Area's geography is the source of its unique weather. It's a place of collisions: tectonic plates, bays and rivers, winds. The Pacific and North American plates collided—are colliding—and created mountains. Two hundred miles inland, the Sierra Nevada range rises up to fourteen thousand feet above sea level. Clouds develop over the ocean and get caught along their eastbound flight by the Sierra's granite peaks. Moisture falls from the clouds below as rain and snow. Creeks and streams and rivers—the Sacramento, the San Joaquin— form and flow toward the ocean.

To the west, the Coast Range overlooks the Pacific below it. Smaller than the Sierra, though no less beautiful in the right light, the Coast Range runs most of the length of California. Between San Francisco and the Marin Headlands, the Sacramento River flows down from the Sierra, carving a gorge through the Coast Range: the Golden Gate Strait.

During the last ice age, glaciers covered most of North America. When the glaciers melted, as the ice age ended, sea levels rose dramatically. Water flowed backward through the Golden Gate and flooded an inland valley, creating the San Francisco Bay.

Out beyond the Coast Range, between it and the Sierra, is the Central Valley, fifty miles wide and five hundred miles long. Freezing cold in the winter and sweat-inducing in the summer, the Valley is home to California's vast agricultural industry. It is also the source of the heat that helps bring the fog to life in coastal San Francisco each summer.

The Pacific High

Most of the sun's energy hits the earth near the equator, where it warms the air. The rays also warm the water, and, through evaporation, moisture fills the air. This warm, moist air rises up into the atmosphere. As it rises, it cools. It then drifts away from the equator, a consequence of the earth's spinning. Out in the Pacific, between San Francisco and the Hawaiian Islands, some of this newly cooled, dense air drops down toward the ocean. This is the Pacific High, a high-pressure system that shifts north and south with the seasons and has significant influence over San Francisco's weather.

Cool winds spread out across the ocean from the Pacific High, seeking low pressure. When they reach California, the winds hit the Coast Range, which stops—or at least slows—the winds' progress. As spring advances, and the sun's path in the sky moves north, the Pacific High gets ever closer to San Francisco. The Central Valley's air warms, creating low pressure inland, which draws the cold, foggy ocean air through San Francisco.

The California Current

The winds that blow against the coast create ocean currents that follow the same northwest-to-southeast path as the wind. The water, like the air, is subject to the Coriolis effect, which shifts these surface ocean currents south. In its place, deep water rises up to the surface. This nutrient-rich upwelling water, often called the California Current, supports an impressive array of sea life, as well as seabirds. It's also shockingly cold. Many a would-be swimmer here, with TV images of California beaches in their heads, steps into San Francisco's ocean water only to run away half frozen.

The Fog Develops

Out of the northwest, the winds blow across the Pacific. Over thousands of miles, they pick up large quantities of evaporated moisture, which is held in the air as invisible water vapor. As it nears the coast, the wind comes into contact with the California Current below. The air cools, and the invisible water vapor condenses. Water droplets form around tiny salt particles that have been kicked off the ocean and into the air. A haze develops off the coast. As more droplets form, the haze becomes fog. The process accelerates as the Central Valley grows hotter and hotter through the summer and the temperature differential between the coast and the Valley increases. The haze seen creeping up the Golden Gate in April is thick fog by late July.

The fog lingers on the coast before advancing into coastal canyons in the afternoon and evening when the sun's rays are weak. Eventually, the fog meets the high ridges, and its progress is halted. On the leeward side of the hills, only a trace of the billowing fog can be seen from a distance. At the Golden Gate, however, the fog is welcomed into the bay. This strait is the only coastal gap in the area where the wind has free rein from sea to sky.

Fog Cycles

Though the fog sometimes seems omnipresent in the Sunset District, in other parts of the Bay Area it comes and goes throughout the summer. It may stay a day, or a few days, or a week. Far inland, there is no fog at all.

The daily fog cycle begins in the early afternoon when fog gathers along the coast and moves inland through the Golden Gate and other gaps, before sitting over the Bay Area during the cool of night. When the sun rises the next day, the fog begins to burn off from above, though traces may remain into the beginning of the next cycle. The daily fog cycle is most evident at the edges of the main fog bank.

At the beginning of the weekly fog cycle, this edge hovers over the coastline. As the weekly cycle plays out, the edge extends further and further inland as the fog covers more and more land. At the height of the weekly cycle, the whole Bay Area may be fogged in for days at a time. At that point in the cycle, the daily cycle moves to the eastern edges of the fog bank. At night, the fog may penetrate all the way to Napa and San Jose, though it will burn off when the sun hits it in the morning.

In the Central Valley, the temperature can reach triple digits during the height of summer. The Pacific High is as close to San Francisco as it will get. Upwelling is at its most intense. Off San Francisco's coast, the conditions are perfect for moisture in the air to condense into the year's thickest fog bank. It moves though mountain gaps, and much of the Bay Area experiences fog—it even reaches the cities of Stockton and Sacramento on some summer nights. And yet, as strong as the fog is, days or weeks will go by without fog forming anywhere but the coast. But why?

One explanation for the weekly cycle is that the process that creates the fog also turns it off, like an emergency valve that keeps the inland areas mostly fog-free. At the height of the fog cycle, the wind and fog are strong enough to penetrate past the hills and the bay, through the Carquinez Strait and into the Central Valley. Once there, the cool ocean air can affect the weather enough to push the temperature down from the triple digits into the nineties for several days. The cool, dense air sits in the Valley rather than rising, reducing the temperature differential and the pressure gradient, which turns off the fog on the coast.

Once the fog stops moving in, the Valley again heats up as the sun shines down. The farmworkers work the fields in the hottest temperatures of the year. The hot air rises and the atmospheric pressure lowers, drawing coastal air back up the Carquinez Strait. The switch has been turned back on. The cool, moist ocean air again flows into the Golden Gate and the bay. At night, it moves up the Carquinez Strait toward the Valley.

The fog returns, the cycle repeats itself.

28

IN THE DISTRICT COURT OF HASKELL COUNTY, KANSAS

PROBATE DIVISION

In the Matter of the Adoption
Of Baby Boy Boelte   Case No. 149

DECREE OF ADOPTION

On this the 28th day of March, 1979, the above entitled matter comes for the hearing before the court upon the petition of Kenneth and Kathleen M. Boelte, being husband and wife, for a final order and decree of the court permitting them to adopt as their own child one baby boy. The parties appear as follows:

The child, Kristopher Bryce Boelte, appears in person along with the Petitioners, Kenneth and Kathleen M. Boelte in person.

The court finds that due and proper notice of the time and place of the hearing of the petition has been given to all persons and parties entitled thereof, that the order of the court requiring notice to be given has been fully complied with, and that proof of the said notice and the service thereof has been duly made and filed in said court; that the mother of said child has duly executed her consent to the adoption of said child by the petitioners, and that there is no other person of whom consent is required or whom notice is required. The court further finds that the consent of such a mother is duly acknowledged as provided by law, and was freely and voluntarily made and that it is filed in this court.

The court further finds that the petitioners are persons of good moral character and reputable standing in the community, and are possessed of sufficient means and ability to maintain and educate said child properly; that the best interest of the said child will be promoted by said adoption, and that said child is suitable for adoption, and all of the provisions of law relative to adoption have been compiled with to the extent that an order and decree ought to be entered.

IT IS THEREFORE BY THE COURT ORDERED AND DECREED that the adoption of Kristopher Bryce Boelte, by Kathleen M. Boelte and Kenneth Boelte, husband and wife, be and it is hereby granted; that the said child is herby adopted as the child of said petitioners.

29

Mom and Dad were married on November 30, 1974. Four years later, in 1978, they were still childless. So they began to let some of their former law school classmates in Oklahoma know that they were thinking about adopting a child.

In November of that year, a classmate living in a small town south of Oklahoma City called their office in Kansas where Mom was working. He had a client—a doctor—who was working with a patient who was pregnant. She was a young woman from a prominent family in a small town in Oklahoma, Mom was told. She was in college now. Earlier that year, she had broken up with her boyfriend. On the rebound, she had slept with another young man. A one-night stand. She had become pregnant.

"Are you and Kenn interested in adopting the girl's child?" their friend asked. "A baby boy."

Dad was heading to Wichita, four hours away, for a meeting. On his way, he picked up a colleague at his brick ranch-style home in Liberal, Kansas. Mom had called the colleague's house and left a message with his wife. When Dad arrived, he got the message and returned Mom's call.

"A baby boy is up for adoption," she said. "We don't have much time. We need to get back to them soon. What do you think?"

He was stunned. They both were. They each needed to think about it. He would call her back when he reached Wichita.

Dad met his colleague's wife and teenage daughter. They were beautiful, the mother and daughter. They looked so much alike, Dad thought. In the car, on the way to Wichita, as they passed field after field of winter wheat, Dad told his colleague that he might be able to adopt a baby boy from Oklahoma. The man was excited for him. He said that both of his children had been adopted.

"I would have never guessed your daughter was adopted," Dad said, surprised. "She looks so much like your wife."

When Dad got to a phone in Wichita, he called Mom and said he thought they should do it. They should adopt the baby boy. She agreed.

Their law partner's wife was a pilot. She flew a twin-engine Beech-craft Bonanza and she too was excited about the adoption. She offered to fly them down to Oklahoma City, where the young woman was in labor. Dad returned from Wichita. They flew down to Oklahoma City on November 9, a clear fall day. The ride was smooth. The high plains stretched in every direction below them.

They assumed that they would fly home the same day. But once on the ground, they found out that they needed the permission of the Oklahoma Department of Human Services to take the baby across state lines. This law hadn't been covered in their classes. The Interstate Compact prevented adopted children from being taken out of state without state permission. They went to the law office where Mom had interned during law school. A classmate who now worked for the firm was able to get the state's permission.

The girl's family insisted that the adoption be confidential. Mom and Dad's friend had emphasized that she was the daughter of a prominent small-town family. Which could mean, Mom and Dad knew, either that they were nationally renowned or perhaps simply owned the local Ford dealership. They were to meet the girl's doctor in the parking lot of a Steak and Ale restaurant. Mom and Dad were always early for everything, and this meeting was no exception. They waited in the car, an old Oldsmobile they had borrowed from Dad's aunt, but no one showed up. They started to worry that there was a problem getting the baby released from the hospital, or that they had misunderstood the doctor in some way when they had talked to him on the phone, or that the girl had changed her mind.

They had tried to get the young woman's medical background, but were told simply that there was nothing significant to report. They knew nothing about the father—the girl herself might not have known much about him either, they thought, given the circumstances. Unwed fathers had no rights in such matters at the time. A woman could put a newborn child up for adoption without the consent or knowledge of the father. Mom and Dad waited in the car for the doctor to arrive while a cold wind blew across the plains.

They wondered why they were meeting the doctor in this parking lot. Why weren't they meeting him at his office?

Finally the doctor pulled up. He stepped out of his Cadillac and approached them. He was middle-aged, with trim gray hair, and he wore a nice suit. He gave them the hospital certificate of birth with the baby's footprints on it. The doctor had torn the hospital's name off the certificate to keep it secret. The baby was wrapped in a soft white hospital blanket. When they unwrapped the baby later, they saw the hospital's name was on the blanket. The doctor must have missed it in his attempt to maintain total secrecy. He handed the baby to Mom.

Beneath the blanket, the baby's umbilical cord was still attached. The doctor did not tell them this was normal. They were left to wonder about it after he left. They had not been preparing for a baby. Not yet. No books or classes. They had thought they would have plenty of time for that. These things tend to take time to arrange, they had thought. Then came the call from their friend. A baby boy was available. They had flown to Oklahoma just a couple of days later. Now they held the baby boy in their hands.

The doctor had only one piece of advice for the new parents. If the baby cried, drive him around in the car. Most babies will fall asleep if you do that, he said. Then he got back into his Cadillac and disappeared.

30

IT'S SUNNY IN SAN Francisco today. Blue skies, warm weather. Earlier this morning, I walked along Laguna Honda, on the west side of Twin Peaks, and watched the clouds circling the hills above me. They soon burned off, so I walked home in the warmth of the sun.

I'm looking through scientific papers now. It's as close as I'll get to fog today. "Geographic Description of Three Fog Ecosystems in the Atacama Coastal Desert of Chile." "Fog Deposition to a Tillandsia Carpet in the Atacama Desert." What do I hope to learn from these collected facts? I have a pile of fog papers in one corner of the house. A pile of Kris's papers in another.

I look away from the papers and out the window. Sunshine. Blue skies. I try to imagine the fog rising off the Pacific into the Cordillera de la Costa. Life-supporting fog. Wisps at first. Then a full bank of fog. It collects on the lichen that envelop the cactus dotting the hills above the coast. I struggle to convert dry facts on paper into meaningful experience.

· · ·

THE ATACAMA DESERT, ON Chile's northwest coast, is one of the driest places on earth. Inhospitable to life, it's often said. The desert plateau stretches almost a thousand miles, from near Arica in the north to near La Serena in the south. At its broadest, it's only one hundred miles across. Much of it is bare rock and sand. Endless miles of nothing. To the east rise the massive Andes Mountains. To the west, the Pacific Ocean. Average precipitation is less than two millimeters a year. In some places, rain has never been observed. Few animals or plants can survive in this harsh environment.

Most life in the Atacama is dependent on coastal fog that materializes over the Pacific Ocean. Coastal mountains and seaside cliffs rise above the ocean, where they catch the fog as it moves inland. The cordillera is made up of limestone and sandstone hills, small mountains and plateaus, thirty miles wide, a thin slice of the Atacama topography, between the ocean and an inland valley at the foot of the Andes. Most of the fog is trapped by the cordillera, though it also slips into the interior through gaps in the hills. The fog zones are on the coastline and on the windward—the south and southwest—side of the hills farther inland.

The advection fog in the Atacama is caused by forces similar to San Francisco's fog. A subtropical high-pressure system, the South Pacific High, sits over the ocean to the west of Chile. This high pressure meets the upwellings of the Humboldt Current, which carries cold water north from Antarctica. When fog forms, it is trapped by an inversion layer, which forces the fog inland until it meets the Cordillera de la Costa and the plants that rely on it for survival.

Much of the plant life in the Atacama is endemic—it is found nowhere else on earth. These plants and animals have adapted to the isolated islands of fog-shrouded land, the *lomas*, which dot the cordillera. Where plants are able to survive, they tend to be cactus and shrubs. Lichen that blanket the cactus pull fog from the air and make it available to other desert inhabitants. Hummingbirds, the Peruvian song sparrow, white-throated earthcreeper, and other birds can be found here, at least for part of the year. Insects, lizards, mice, foxes, and guanaco—South American camels—live in small numbers in the *lomas*. The fog breathes life into the landscape.

. . .

THE FIRST PEOPLE TO settle the Atacama Desert arrived ten thousand to eleven thousand years ago. They predated agriculture, but they do not fit the popular image of hunter-gatherers. They were sedentary fishing people in a place where it would have been extremely difficult to be nomadic. Unlike most everything else that lives in the Atacama, humans were able to survive in this desert without relying directly on the fog, though they must have lived much of their lives inside it.

The paper now in front of me is "Chinchorro Culture: Pioneers of the Coast of the Atacama Desert," by Bernardo T. Arriaza and his colleagues. As I read about the Chinchorro, I imagine a young man tracing the ridges of the cordillera in the early morning fog. *What is this fog that envelops our world?* he too wonders, as it overtakes the land.

I've come across this digression by accident while searching for information about fog in the Atacama. Weeks ago I came across an introductory speech Kris gave to his new classmates at Highlands Ranch High. I was looking through his schoolwork when I found it. How should I view the speech? What should I make of it?

I imagine Kris standing up from his desk and walking up to the front of the class. He's nervous. Pretends not to be.

"My name is Kris Boelte and I'm a sophomore," he says. His eyes dart around the room. "If I had to describe myself, I would say that I'm pretty unlucky . . ."

The fog swirls on the edge of the Atacama. Words on paper begin to take life.

"I live with both my parents, Kenn and Kathy, who decided that it would be cute to have all my family's names begin with *K*," he tells the class. "So when my younger brother was born they named him Kyle. So now I'm stuck with a family whose names are Kenn, Kathy, Kris, and Kyle."

The speech is short, a few selected facts and stories from his life.

"I also have a dog named Shanghai who is pretty stupid and spends most of his time running into things," he says casually. He's relieved to hear muted laugher rising from the desks in front of him.

"That's basically my life," he says in closing. "All the other stuff would probably put you to sleep, if this already hasn't."

He pauses, manages a smile, and takes his seat. I return to the desert.

Two factors allowed the settlement of the Atacama. Rivers that cut through the cordillera from the Andes provided an oasis in an otherwise parched landscape, and the upwelling of water in the Pacific to the west provided a rich diversity of marine life. This combination of isolated freshwater and dependable food made the Atacama—more accurately, a few small pockets on the edge of the Atacama—a surprisingly good place to settle down.

Early settlers relied on simple technologies—wooden or bone harpoons, fishing hooks made of cactus needles—to make a living from the sea. They did not yet have ceramics, but they made use of reeds to make baskets, clothes, and cords. Though long-term survival itself in such a seemingly inhospitable environment is noteworthy, the Chinchorros are best known—if they are known at all—for the mummification of their dead.

"The Chinchorros transformed their dead into highly artistic mortuary icons, epitomized by the so-called black and red mummies," writes Arriaza.

They did this for several millennia. The styles changed over time, but the drive to create something beautiful remained the same.

The black mummies were the result of a complex process. Morticians buried the body in a swampy area to be later exhumed. Then they cleaned the bones and flesh and replaced the brain and internal organs with grasses and clay. Thin wooden poles, stretched from head to foot and tied with reeds, gave the body structure. The organs, even genitals, were re-created out of gray clay. In this way, the individuality of the deceased was brought back to life.

"The morticians worked meticulously and must have possessed great anatomical knowledge since bones are in proper anatomical positions," writes Arriaza.

They most likely set aside some of the original skin before the first burial. After the body was disinterred and cleaned and stuffed, the morticians would reapply the skin to the stuffed body, using seal or sea lion skin to supplement the original if needed. A short black wig adorned the head. The body was painted with a black-blue manganese paste.

The mummies became simpler over time, and more beautiful. Researchers refer to black mummies and the red mummies that followed them. The style of mummification changed, but the belief that the dead could be reanimated remained for several thousand years.

Why go to all this trouble, one wonders.

The mummy wasn't just a dead body that had been dried and painted. The dead were resurrected through the intricate work of the morticians. The line between life and death was not so clear. The Chinchorro knew their dead as they knew their living. The dead continued to live, even—at least long enough, perhaps, to make the journey to the afterworld. Mummification allowed the Chinchorro to breathe life into their dead.

Kris was cremated soon after he was found. He was buried in a cemetery in south Denver overlooking the mountains. In high school, I would sometimes visit his grave and talk to him. I would ask him questions as I looked out over the mountains rising to the west. I wouldn't tell anyone I was going to the cemetery. I'd go by myself and shed tears alone, with Kris, my questions floating on the wind.

31

INTRODUCTORY SPEECH
KRIS BOELTE

My name is Kris Boelte and I'm a sophomore. If I had to describe myself I would say that I'm pretty unlucky. My bad luck started last year when I was riding on the hood of a friends jeep as a joke. Well it turned out to not be as funny as we thought it would be. As he was turning the corner at the end of the street I slipped off and my left foot went directly under the front tire and smashed it. I was in shock for about two minutes when I realized I was having a hard time walking. The result of my accident was three fractures in my foot and the cartilage had been blown out of my second toe, which required surgery. But this wasn't the extent of the damage I hadn't dealt with my parents yet. They thought a good punishment was for me to be grounded for a long time and not be able to drive till my second term of my sophomore year. I also spent a lot of time doing hard labor at the dog pound during the summer as the result of an unrelated incident. It would have been an o.k. job if you don't mind shoveling dog feces and walking sick and demented animals for eight hours. As far as my personal life goes I moved here from Kansas four years ago and have been attending school at Colorado Academy for the past two years. I spend my free time playing baseball, and playing the drums. When I not doing that stuff I usually hang out with friends. I haven't decided what I want to do with the rest of my life, except I'm pretty sure I want to go to Collage and get a good enough education to get a good job and make myself rich. I guess I should mention my family to. I live with both my parents Kenn and Kathy who decided that it would be cute to have all my families names begin with k. So when my younger brother was born they named him Kyle. So now I'm stuck with a family who's names are Kenn, Kathy, Kris and Kyle. I also have a dog named shanghai who is pretty stupid and spends most of his time running into things. My favorite types of music are rap and alternative and an occasional mix of heavy metal. My parents despise my taste in music but I'd rather listen to my music than my parents over the hill classics. Thats basically my life all the other stuff would probably put you to sleep if this allready hasn't. Thank you.

32

THE SUN FILTERS THROUGH the green canopy above. Beams of light illuminate the forest at random intervals. Shadows are everywhere. The sky visible through the tangle of tree branches is bright blue. The morning sun has burned off any trace of fog.

"We need to set up ten plots," Dr. Emily Burns, a plant ecologist who studies fog in redwood forests, tells two research assistants. A few months ago, I came across one of her studies, which describes how redwoods and other plants in the redwood forest can absorb water from the fog. I wanted to know more about these trees that pull water from the sky. I contacted Dr. Burns to ask her about her fog research, and she invited me to join her team in a forest on the west side of Marin for a day.

As we watch the assistants scramble up the hill, I ask Dr. Burns what people make of the fact that she studies fog.

"People tend to have negative associations with the word *fog*," she tells me. She grew up in Marin County and has been living with the fog for most of her life. "One thing I really like about talking to the public is showing them that fog can be a good thing. The redwoods rely on fog, after all."

Redwoods are the tallest trees in the world. An evergreen conifer and member of the cypress family, the redwood is an ancient species. It once grew throughout North America, all the way up to the Arctic. That was millions of years ago, when the climate was much warmer and wetter. But over time, as the world cooled and glaciers grew across the continent, the redwood forest retreated to the coast of California. By the time humans appeared in North America, redwoods remained only in a thin strip along the West Coast from what is now Big Sur up to the Oregon border. Not coincidentally, the redwood forests overlap with the fog zones of the Pacific coast.

Summer is the growing season for most plants here, but little rain falls on the California coast in the summer months. The redwood forest, without access to summer rain, has come to depend on the fog. Each summer, as the fog moves across the Coast Range, it comes upon redwood groves and is caught by the towering trees. The moisture condenses on branches and falls to the forest floor, drop by drop. About a fifth of the water inside redwood trees during the summer has been absorbed from fog in the air; the rest is from groundwater.

In the understory, small plants like the sword fern are even more reliant on the fog than the redwoods are. Their roots are too short to reach the water table. They rely on the fog that drips down onto the ground cover to make it through the dry summer. Up to two-thirds of the water these plants use comes from fog. Redwoods, in addition to capturing fog, also protect the forest floor from direct sunlight, reducing evaporation and keeping the floor moist.

Many of the redwoods growing today have been living in the summer fog for hundreds of years. Some individuals, the giants that rise as much as 380 feet off the forest floor, are two thousand years old or more. Logging has wiped out most of the ancient coast redwoods. Ninety-five percent of the old-growth redwoods have been felled in the past two hundred years. After the 1906 earthquake destroyed much of San Francisco, the city was rebuilt with redwoods from Marin County. Now, only a small fraction of the old-growth redwoods survive along the coast.

Fog is now a lifeline for the redwood forest, one that allows it to survive as the climate becomes hotter and drier.

I climb up the slope while the assistants count out their measurements and Dr. Burns takes notes. I lean against a moss-covered tree, facing uphill, and stare up at the towering redwoods above me.

"I've got thirty-four fronds on number one," one assistant begins. I look down from the treetops to the slow rhythm of data collection around me. "I've got three fronds, lengths seventy-six, seventy-nine, seventy-five." This is how science is done, steady observation and data collection.

As Dr. Burns works, we talk about her research. How does being in the field, experiencing fog firsthand, relate to the final product, the published paper? I ask.

"It's very immediate in the field," she says, "and only becomes more abstract later back in the office. Fog is incredibly beautiful in the forest. Sometimes it beads up, and the leaves have a constant wetness. I love to photograph leaves when they are covered with beads of water from the fog."

She continues to measure the traces of fog from the fern fronds, sitting in the shadows of the giant redwood towering above us.

"I tried to chase fog for six years and failed," she says. "I wanted to take measurements before and after fog events to see how the forest was affected. But you cannot really predict when it's coming, how many days it will last, or when it will burn off."

"Are you trying to predict it?" I ask.

"Our big motivation is that we want to predict it," she tells me. "In our work, as scientists who take measurements, it's hard to know when to feel comfortable making a prediction from the data. But that is the goal."

She takes a reading, and one of the assistants jots it down.

"I could guess how hydrated a fern is, for example. I've seen enough examples to anticipate the results I will get when I take measurements. To make accurate predictions, we'd have to understand how the plants affect the climate, and what will happen to the plants as the climate changes. There are all these complicated factors that make prediction elusive."

Dr. Burns grows quiet, meditative. Her voice softens as she speaks.

"The marbled murrelet is a seabird that fishes in the Pacific and builds its nest in the redwoods," she muses. "It lays one egg on a branch, that's all. No one knew it was doing this for years. They couldn't see it happening."

The trees towering above us sway in the breeze.

"Only in the sixties did people find out that it was doing this. Foresters had called them 'fog larks' because they could hear them but couldn't see them."

Shadows dance across the ground in front of us.

"So much still remains out of sight."

33

What is it like to be a teenager? To feel life coming straight at you, everything moving too fast, the heart chaotic? When a girl is not just a girl.

There is a photograph, from Kris's box, of a girl in a Highlands Ranch High School cheerleading uniform. She is a senior. Blue eyes. Blonde hair that flows past her shoulders. The uniform is blue and black with FALCONS written across the front of the long-sleeve top. Below her skirt: thigh, knees, legs shaved and tanned. Her hands are on her hips. Her elbows out. She smiles. She looks happy.

Kris had met her through a friend. Had she babysat for the friend at some point? It sounds right but I may be confusing things. I hadn't thought about her much in ten or fifteen years. I once knew of her—I don't think I ever met her—but then she slipped into a stream of vanishing memories. I pick up the photograph now and look at it and remember.

She was older. In her first year of college in the fall of 1994. They had met the previous summer.

What is it like to be a teenager? To be confused. Everything new and real and immediate. What is sex and love and feeling? What is it that we crave?

She signed in at the memorial service. Near the end of the list of attendees. I came across the name recently as I flipped through the small book. What was she feeling as she signed in, she who had signed up for a little fun with a younger guy—tall, broad shouldered, dark hair, and funny—and was now at his memorial service? She, who like

us all, was not responsible but was there and played a part before the
final act.

Aug 21, 1994
Sunday

Kris,

Hey sweets! What is ↑? I hope that school is
okay! How is Tim? I miss you! Well I ended up
pledging Tri Delt. It is an awesome house. I have been
drunk for the last three nights. Classes start tomorrow,
yuk. What teachers do you have? I'm sure I've had
some of them. High school just blows! I miss the cheer-
leaders! You are going to be sick of seeing them in
uniform. I think I only wore regular clothes 1 time a
week. Well I'm sure you care! I found a roomate the
first day I moved in. Her name is Melanie. She kinda
looks like me but we act alot alike also. We have a
good time! I miss Colorado. It's so <u>hot</u> here! Oh well. I
really miss the mountains! Well I'm doing my laundry
so I'm gonna let you go!

Love,
Kimberly   W/B ☺

Kris,

What's ↑? I bet you thought I had died ☺ J/K.
I am sooo busy. I ♥ getting letters from you. It's just
that I don't have very much time to write to you. I feel
bad, but what can I do? KU is so awesome you will
♥ it rocks! ☺ Seriously though I am so happy that
I chose to come here. Classes are hard! I ♥ mine but
they are hard! I had Mr. Baker. I ♥ him tell him

I said "hi" he will know who I am. He is sooo cool!
Please continue to write to me. It's so nice to get mail!
☺ Plus your letters always cheer me ↑. I need to go,
but I hope that all is well! I miss you & hope you are
taking care of your body! I'm not doing so well w/
that but oh well! Take it easy! 🖤 ☺ I won't probably
be home until Nov. Even then I'm gonna be busy, but
I'll try to come see you. Study hard!
                                        Love,
                                        Kimberly   W/B ☺

Kris,
    Hey Bud! What's up? Not much is new here. Hey
um I need to talk w/ you & since I have no calling
card I can't do it by phone, but anyways –
    I'm a little upset at either you or Bobby but it's
pretty embarrassing when Tim calls me and says that
you are lusting after me and waiting to spend time
with only me. I told you before I left that I would
not really be waiting around. I mean I really think
you are a great guy & I love hearing from you all the
time. I don't care if you write or anything, but I don't
really need a reputation @ H.R. even after I'm gone.
I hate it there I don't ever want to go back. H.R. is
awful!! In fact I'm only going home for a little while
over summer break. I'm going to summer school & going
to get a job. I can't come home at all unless it's for
like a week. This makes me sooo sad. Oh well. I 🖤
getting notes from you and also to hear how you are
– anyways –
    I'm sorry that things aren't going good between
you & your parents – that sucks. I do know how it is

trust me! High school is hard, but just wait college is even harder! I'm serious it just sucks! I hate all the reading I have to do & all of the shit we do it really does suck!

Well anyways I hope that all is well! I'm gonna go now! I miss you, take care & have fun.

Later,
Kimberly

Nov 13th
8:46pm

Kris,

Hey! What's ↑? I got your letter today! Even though it's a Sunday! ☺ I'm sorry to hear things are not going to well at home. It will get better though! School is hard too! Bio. is my favorite course so if you need help you can call me. I'm sure you probably can't call me, but if you can I'll help. I mainly wrote to you to tell you that I moved to a different dorm. I got so sick of my roomate so I moved. So my new address is ~

420 West 11th St.
Lawrence, Kansas
66045

So now you can write me as much as you want! I'll try to write you back as soon as possible. Anyways I'm going to let you go. I'll see you soon!

Love,
Kimberly

. . .

WHAT IS SEX AND love and feeling? At sixteen, to feel close to someone. To belong, in the moments you are together, to share your insecurities, your secrets, your hidden self. To share your breath.

What is it like to be a teenager, so fake and foolish but wanting so much to look real—to be real. A teenager who does not belong. Who no one wanted. Who is not good enough, not smart enough, not athletic enough. How does it feel to be a teenager? When feeling is everything. When feeling is life itself.

Who meets a girl, a cheerleader no less. Blonde. Tanned legs. And older. Who has sex. Makes love? Fools around. Who feels the power to attract, to belong.

The feeling is real, so real. So much realer than anything else. School and baseball. Friends and drugs.

Fitting in, standing out, being someone. And then this. Clothes in a pile beside the bed. Skin against skin. This moment. This.

It comes in waves. It is real in the moment and then it fades with distance. It is real when it is felt, and then distant in contemplation. It is real when it is stripped down, human flesh, closeness, shared breath. And then the waiting, always the waiting, for the next moment as this one disappears into the past.

34

"I promise nothing complete," writes Melville, in his essay on whales, "because any human thing supposed to be complete, must for that very reason infallibly be faulty."

What is a fact? Something real, something solid, something that can be named and pointed to. A guidebook adds facts up, provides an explanation, points with certainty. Yet it can only hint at the world's complexities.

Behind the scenes, scientists argue about what is truly happening. They voice disagreements at conferences; they pound them out on keyboards. A guidebook chooses theories, models, hypotheses to represent the world. It subdues nature, controls the facts, presents a clear story.

Fog comes to life through perspective. When it soars high above your head it is a cloud. When it surrounds, engulfs, overwhelms you: it is fog.

Fog is fog only when you are inside of it.

35

THE WEEKLY FOG CYCLE model is compellingly simple. Cold, upwelled ocean water; high pressure off the coast; heat and low pressure over the Central Valley. The fog builds over San Francisco; the fog enters the Central Valley; the Valley cools; the fog mechanism weakens until the Valley warms up again. The cycle repeats.

But the fog doesn't follow this weekly cycle neatly. Weeks of fog or sunshine can persist in the Bay Area during the summer.

The weekly cycle model explains only what's happening in the air close to the surface of the earth. High in the atmosphere, other forces are at work. Forces that the weekly cycle doesn't account for.

On a round-trip flight across the United States, the eastbound leg will be faster than the westbound leg. This is due to the polar jet stream in the Northern Hemisphere, a set of fast currents of air flowing west to east at 150 miles an hour or more. These currents, roughly thirty thousand feet above the ground, are caused by the rotation of the earth and by solar heating. The jet streams of the Northern and Southern Hemispheres are influenced by the Coriolis effect and tend to meander north- and southward, rather than flowing directly eastward around the globe.

There are two jet streams in each hemisphere: the polar and the subtropical. The polar jet stream most affects the weather of the United States, and, like the Pacific High, it moves north in the summer and south in the winter. And though it is centered over Canada in the summer, the polar jet stream influences the fog in the Bay Area thousands of miles to the south.

Associated with the jet stream's shifts in direction are atmospheric pressure waves, ridges and troughs of high and low pressure, which travel north and south from the path of the jet stream. The ridges of high pressure bring clear weather, and the troughs of low pressure tend to bring storms. When a trough is over Canada in the summer, the sky will open up there and rain will fall. The ridges and troughs also reach south to affect the California coast from high above.

The coastal fog cycle is dependent on the pressure differential between the coast and inland valleys. The jet stream complicates the cycle by exerting its own pressure. When a ridge of low pressure moves south over the Pacific Ocean west of San Francisco, it reduces the strength of the Pacific High. The winds that create the fog die down, and the Bay Area is clear. Likewise, a ridge of high pressure moving down over the Pacific can strengthen the Pacific High, intensifying fog production. The ridges and troughs are part of the same wave. When a low-pressure trough moves from ocean to land, a high-pressure ridge takes its place over the ocean. There is no weekly fog cycle, not strictly speaking.

Summer is not the only time that fog forms around San Francisco. In winter, the coastal weather pattern that developed in the summer reverses, and a new kind of fog develops: tule fog.

Winter is the wet season in California. In the Sierra that means snow, but in the lower valleys, moisture comes mostly in the form of rain. After the rains, when the ground is soaked with water, the air can pick up much of that water in the form of water vapor. Then, during the long, cold winter nights, the temperature can drop enough to reach the dew point, and the vapor condenses into fog.

Tule fog often forms inland, in the Sacramento–San Joaquin River Delta, but it can creep into the bay through gaps in the Coast Range, reversing the flow found during the summer. Less often, when coastal temperatures plunge, tule fog forms low over the bay itself before spilling out into the ocean through the Golden Gate.

The SS *City of Rio de Janeiro* sank near Fort Point, in February 1901, in tule fog.

Many of the ships that have sunk near San Francisco sank not during the summer fog season, but rather in winter during a thick tule fog.

Then there are times when it all falls apart. The trade winds stop blowing to the west. The monsoons in Asia are replaced with drought. The upwelling of cold water off the west coasts of Peru and California halts, and relatively warm surface waters remain. The Pacific High does not form, and a low-pressure system sits over the ocean, near Tahiti. Warm air and water off the California coast lead to more evaporation of water off the ocean's surface and more rain onshore. The low pressure coming down from Canada brings the jet stream south, so that it now flows over the Bay Area. Rains follow. Rain and then clear days cycle with the jet stream's ridges and troughs. The fog is gone, its mechanism broken down. El Niño has arrived.

El Niño events happen every four to seven years. They have dramatic effects on millions of people. Drought and floods are felt across large stretches of land. Fishermen struggle when the upwelling zones disappear and the rich fisheries that come with them vanish. Life that depends on the fog must survive without it or perish.

Attempts to predict El Niño—and La Niña, an intensification of normal conditions—are made. But predictions work only in the short term, and even so, El Niño predictions are often wrong. Like many of the mechanisms that affect the fog, in the final analysis these events are not well understood.

Some researchers cite chaos theory, which postulates that tiny differences in initial conditions can result in radically different outcomes. Other theories exist.

The immediate cause of El Niño and La Niña is a change in pressure over the Pacific Ocean. And the cause of that cause? It's unclear.

36

Dear Kyle, Kenn, and Kathy,

Enclosed is a copy of my eulogy for Kris.

I hope that this and many other things will serve to help you make this loss bearable, at least.

Please call me—For Any Reason.

James

WE WATCHED THE MEMORIAL service from a family viewing area, off to the side of the main room. We watched through wooden slats, our vision partially obscured, away from the crowd who came to share our grief. We were invisible to the main room.

A friend later asked, "Where were you? I didn't see you." I was behind the wooden slats, I told him, where we could not be seen. Behind the wooden slats, where our field of vision was incomplete. I saw the service as I saw much of life in the days after Kris's death. The swirled movement, the distant voices.

> But soon we shall die and all memory of those five will have left the earth, and we ourselves shall be loved for a while and forgotten. But the love will have been enough; all those impulses of love return to the love that made them. Even memory is not necessary for love. There is a land of the living and a land of the dead and the bridge is love, the only survival, the only meaning.
>
> —THORNTON WILDER

It was standing room only. Two hundred and twenty-eight people signed the guest book. They sat in wooden pews; they stood in the back. They spoke in hushed voices. *What a tragedy. What a tragedy.* As they awaited the eulogy, they looked through the short program. They read a Thornton Wilder quote from *The Bridge of San Luis Rey* that Dad had picked out.

So many people. Friends and teachers, Kris's and mine both. My parents' friends and coworkers. Many I did not know. Our school bus driver, Felix, was there. So many friends.

Hey, you, out there in the cold
Getting lonely, getting old
Can you feel me?
Hey, you, standing in the aisles
With itchy feet and fading smiles
Can you feel me?
Hey, you, don't help them to bury the light
Don't give in without a fight.

Kris's body, drained of life, was not present. His ashes were awaiting burial in the cemetery plot overlooking the mountains. At the front of the memorial service, beside a photo of Kris, and his blue hoodie, and flowers, his friends laid down their own remembrances. Photos. Knickknacks. A Slurpee from 7-Eleven. Inside jokes scribbled on notebook paper. A small table was crowded with small gestures of significance. They seemed odd to me at the time—too little, too ordinary for such a solemn occasion.

How else does a teenager demonstrate love, though, than through the artifacts of the only life they know?

Hey, you, out there on the road
Always doing what you're told,

Can you help me?
Hey, you, out there beyond the wall,
Breaking bottles in the hall,
Can you help me?
Hey, you, don't tell me there's no hope at all
Together we stand, divided we fall

37

A memorial is what we do to remember, and so we gather at this memorial so that we will not forget. What each of us feels now is–it is what it is: in this room there will be feelings of sadness, feelings of anger; there will be feelings of fear, of being afraid; there will be feelings of emptiness, a hollowness in the heart. There may perhaps be some laughter, or deep, deep within our hearts some hope, hope that no one will ever again be lost in the way Kris has been lost to us.

Questions filled the heart of Kristopher Boelte, deeply felt questions, difficult questions. It seems Kris felt these questions–felt them as though they were jewels within his heart, within his mind. Jewels beautiful, jewels painful, too, for what Kris feared most was sharing those beautiful, painful questions with us– that the jewels that were his most precious, painful possession would be taken from him. And now he–and they–he has taken from us.

Kris was born in Oklahoma to biological parents he never knew, and with loving arms two joyous parents, Kathy and Kenn Boelte, created the family that was Kris'.

Kris' parents immediately saw his strong mind and endless curiosity. The blond toddler would listen as his mommy and daddy read books to him, and would repeat those books back to them from his memory.

Kris, the elementary school boy, loved learning, and he used his sharp mind to learn what fascinated him. He loved learning about dinosaurs, and he knew so much about the Deinonychus the Brachiosaurus, the Tyrannosaurus that he was asked to teach the other children in his school. I imagine that his eyes shined with delight when others shared their love of curiosity and learning with him.

Kris loved his brother, Kyle. He told his other friends how he loved Kyle both as a brother and as the best of friends. There are pictures of Kris and Kyle, standing next to each other as brothers who really understand friendship.

Kris' mind expanded tremendously when he became a teenager. Like all of us human beings, he no longer had a child-like acceptance of the values of his parents, of his teachers, or his society. At first he rejected our values, and so he looked to his friends for values.

Kris chose friends who valued friendship—he also chose some friends who valued the defiant glamour of drugs. Drugs are things, though, just chemicals that we can use for good or bad—some drugs, when we chose to use them, can make us feel better, and make us feel happy. There is nothing wrong with feeling happy—it's good to feel happy! But these drugs also take away our minds, and drugs took Kris' wonderful mind, and now we have lost Kris.

Kris was in pain, because he knew he could no longer survive the drugs. But I wonder if by rejecting drugs he became confused with rejecting his friends. If he chose not to party, not to be cool enough to be on drugs at school, did it mean that he might have to reject his friends, too? Kris loved his friends very much, and did not want to leave them. But what Kris didn't know was how wonderful he was, just the way he was when he was sober. Smart, funny, gentle, vulnerable, a nice guy who could ask really hard questions—questions that authority figures really don't like—really they were questions that are really hard for all of us: why are we here? who are we? what are we going to do about it?

But Kris hid these things—he hid his mind—everyone here has discovered this—and this cost him his life. His sharp, deep questions he kept hidden within himself, and hidden there they cut at him, they hurt. He was right to work with a therapist, to try to find a way to use his gifts. But he wouldn't trust. He searched for a safe place to trust, to reveal himself and his questions. He found a few people—Tim, Monica, Justin—friends he almost trusted. It was known to many that Kris became his truest self on Justin's deck, smoking Marlboros and asking questions.

Kris was searching for values. The values that his sharp mind and powerfully profound questions required were too tough for us. People like Kris who are often defiant at simplistic answers to tough questions. But Kris still wanted answers, however, and God—if there is a God—has seen fit only to give a whole bunch of answers—and a lot of those answers are too shallow or too unreasonable for a mind like Kris'.

Values, a kind of answer to tough questions like "why are we here and what are we going to do about it?" values, these answers to questions cannot be taught. We learn them for ourselves. We learn them by living—not by dying. The value of responsibility, for example, cannot be taught—each of us learns that for ourselves. It is learned, usually with difficulty.

It's important to remember in a time like this that when Kris ended his life it was his response—his responsibility—his choosing.

Trust is essential to life, even though every one of us is going to fail each other sometimes. We will sometimes fail a friend's trust, a lover's trust, a child's trust—we're only human, after all. Kris would not trust any of his schoolmates and his parents—without trust he felt he must hide his decision to die from his best friends and family, and without trust he hid his mind in drugs.

Drugs do not hide feelings. Drugs only lose our minds, and Kris lost his mind with them, and so he was killed by his own feelings running senseless through his soul.

This is always true: there will always be a better tomorrow, just as the flowers will always have a Spring to bloom again. Kris chose without his mind, and although his feelings of despair were real, his conclusion that he had no other choice was false. You had so much to live for, Kristopher Boelte, and now what we here on earth have left of you is our memories.

We need Kris, we need him for his gentle loving friendship, for his tough, irritating questions, for his gentle and profound soul. His beautiful eyes showed a deep compassion, complex, interesting feelings and thoughts. It will be a long time before we see someone wearing a black hat with a Colorado Rockies logo and won't immediately think of a young man, hat pulled low, whose gentle soul calls us to the toughest questions and deepest love.

38

THE TERRIFYING THING ABOUT the bridge is the glimmer of recognition when you step near the edge. Not the worry about slipping or being pushed. The knowledge that you have the power to cross over voluntarily. That you are not all that different from those who have.

I look up. The faint curve of the suspension cables fades in and out behind the blowing fog. To the west, beyond the cars and cyclists crossing the bridge, a bright white field of fog is backlit by the afternoon sun. It is a whiteness that makes me think of Arctic explorers stumbling toward safety—the safety of what, up there among all that ice? a native village?—that they will never find, stumbling, stumbling until they must stop, falling to their knees as they stare into an endless blinding whiteness.

There is movement everywhere on the bridge. Tourists crowd it, walking and running and jumping into the air for a photograph. The cars flow past, the rhythm of their wheels over the contours of the pavement drones over and over again. The wind blows, the fog with it. Noise and movement overwhelm.

I'm walking across the east walkway, the side closest to the city. I can't see the city. If I look straight out over the railing, I can see only the erratic white brushstrokes of fog. When I look down over the edge, the water comes into view, 220 feet below. I stay away from the edge. The railing is so short even a young child could easily climb over and fall to the water below. I watch the sky's delicate transfiguration. A thousand different whites.

I don't much like heights. I've spent a lot of time hiking mountain peaks in Colorado, walking carefully across sawtooth ridges. I've never been one to walk right to the edge of a drop-off to peer over, though. I started rock climbing a decade ago. I'd better address this fear while I'm young, I reasoned. But climbing involves harnesses and rope. The bridge offers only this short railing. Wind gusts push me toward it. People pass me on the right and left. Tourists on rented bikes occasionally ride by. Movement everywhere. The wind picks up, and the south tower, fifty feet in front of me, disappears completely.

A little girl in front of me holds on to the railing, steps up onto the low edge, and peers over. She stretches on her tiptoes to see over the four-foot barrier. She looks down.

Most everyone on the bridge stops at some point to look over the edge. Groups of people are standing against the railing peering over. Lone individuals hold on to the railing and stare down. They study the distance to the sea. They stand on the edge, most all of them, at some point. It's impossible to know who among them is preparing for a final leap.

*   *   *

THE GOLDEN GATE BRIDGE is the site of more than a thousand suicides over the past seventy-five years. No other single place has seen more deaths by suicide. The first occurred just three months after the bridge was completed. The short, four-foot railing on the edge of the bridge makes it easy for pedestrians crossing the bridge to jump. The height of the bridge makes a fall from it extremely lethal. The sublimity of the landscape gives the bridge a haunting attraction.

When the number of recorded deaths from the bridge approached 500 in 1973 and then 1,000 in 1995, the Bay Area media launched countdowns and played up the events. Mental health professionals advised the media to downplay jumps from the bridge. They worried that the more people knew about suicides on the bridge, the more people would be drawn to bridge. The media mostly stopped covering the suicides. The California Highway Patrol stopped its official count at 997.

Silence didn't work. Jumps from the bridge continued as before. The railing remained the same height. The landscape remained sublime. The fall just as lethal. The number of recorded suicides from the bridge is now close to 1,600. The actual number is much larger.

A barrier could be built that would prevent such deaths. A taller railing, or more likely, a net below the bridge. Such methods have been used to prevent suicides on other bridges around the world. Opposition to such preventive methods is mainly based on aesthetics. The bridge is an icon, some say. Its beauty unsurpassed the world over. And besides, people who want to die will just kill themselves somewhere else. They are free to do it.

A documentary film crew captured close to two dozen jumps from the bridge on camera in 2004. The recorded jumps were an extreme break in the silence that had surrounded the bridge suicides for decades. Individuals stood on, and paced, and looked over the edge of the bridge before jumping, their bodies falling toward the water 220 feet below. They hit the water as though they were hitting a stone wall. Hitting it with unanticipated force, their ribs snapping, their hearts and lungs tearing, their vertebrae breaking.

39

The sheriff's department has not found a suicide note. However, Denes speculated that, "while (the investigation) may not have directly precipitated the suicide ... it may have had something to do with it."

MOM AND DAD DIDN'T know that Kris was using drugs, though they had disciplined him for drinking. They had never really been around drugs, even when they were young. LSD was something they had read about in newspapers in the sixties, not something they actually knew much about. When they were informed Kris was involved with LSD, they were shocked. LSD was simply not part of their world.

There's a pink sheet of paper in the box. A carbon copy of an evidence inventory filled out after the sheriff's department went through Kris's room while we were at the memorial service. "Non-Criminal" is checked in the top left corner. *Death Investigation* is written under "Offense." DESCRIPTION: *Numerous stamps / blotters.* LOCATION FOUND: *Trunk in Kristopher's room.*

I knew my brother used drugs. He talked about it. He joked about it. At least around other teenagers. I remember Kris once wearing a kid's

Burger King crown at school. The text on the crown, crossed out and rewritten with a Sharpie, said *King Weed*.

Seth—I might run away if I have to. Each day they keep getting closer and closer to my stash. I risk everything writing this down but I needed to tell someone. —Kris

Shane tells me a story I had forgotten. We were at my house, and he and I wandered into Kris's room. Kris told me to leave; he didn't want me to see what he was doing. Shane stayed for a couple of minutes, talking to Kris, who was working with stamps.

Many of the teenagers I grew up with used drugs. Most experimented at some point. Pot, LSD, ecstasy, speed. I never smoked weed or used other illicit drugs. I would politely decline. "I'm good," I would say nonchalantly, as the pipe was passed.

Many of the people I knew who used drugs as teenagers are now doctors and lawyers and other professionals. A friend of mine was kicked out of high school, when we were about sixteen, under suspicion of dealing drugs. He is a successful businessman. His children are beautiful.

Boelte, 16, killed himself Friday. Denes said authorities don't know if the suicide is linked to the investigation.

But the boy's parents, who were not identified, are using his death to warn about drugs, a school official said.

"Kristopher's parents stated that out of this tragedy it is their hope that students will make more positive choices than their son made," said Jill Fox, Douglas County schools spokeswoman.

HIGHLANDS RANCH HIGH SCHOOL
DISCIPLINARY REFERRAL

Student _Kris. Boelts_ Grade _10_ Date _12/16/94_ Time _____

Referring Person _Marten_ Place of Incident _9th Hallway / Drug-Free Zone_

TEACHER RESPONSE
DISCIPLINARY INFRACTIONS

_____ Disruptive Behavior

_____ Verbal Defiance/Disrespect Toward Staff (Swearing/Obscene Language)

_____ Violation of Closed Campus Policy

_____ Harassment/Discrimination

_____ Assault

_____ Destruction of School Property

_____ Accumulation of Infractions

_____ Other _____

_____ Automobile Violation

_____ Insubordinate/Defiance

_____ Possession/Use of Cigarettes, Chew, Matches, Lighter

_____ Skipping Detention

_____ Vandalism

_____ Forgery

_X_ Possession/Distribution/Influence of Drugs/Alcohol/Paraphernalia

_____ Theft

Summary of actions previously taken by teacher: _Exchanged acid to a_

Comments: _student in the 9th grade hallway._

ADMINISTRATIVE ACTION TAKEN

_____ Teacher/Student Conference _____

_____ After-School Detention (2:35-4:40 P.M.) Date/s _____

_____ Other _____

_X_ Parent/Guardian Conference _12/16 7:00_

_X_ Out-of-School Suspension _Jan_ Date/s _12/16, 19, 20, 21 10, 11, 12, 13/6 17_

_____ Parent/Guardian Telephoned

Comments/Next Consequence: _10 additional days requested from Supt. of Schools. Jan 18, 19, 23, 24, 25, 26, 27, 30, 31 request will be made for expulsion hearing Feb 1_

Administrator _Marten_ Student _X Kris Boelts_ Date _12-16-94_

PARENT RESPONSE

Parents/Guardians: Thank you for your cooperation and support of the corrective action initiated today. If you have further questions, please call the administrator who handled this referral at 470-0700.

Parent Comment: _____

_____ Parent signature required if checked by administrator. Student must return signed referral to the Main Office by 7:30 a.m. the following day.

Parent Signature _Kathleen M. Boelts_ Date _12-16-94_

Parent's Copy - White   Teacher's Copy - Yellow   Office Copy - Pink

40

LYSERGIC ACID DIETHYLAMIDE WAS first synthesized in 1938 by Dr. Albert Hofmann, of Sandoz Pharmaceuticals, in Basel, Switzerland. He had been investigating the pharmacological properties of ergot, a rye fungus. "Ergot, more than any other drug, has a fascinating history," he later wrote, "in the course of which its role and meaning have been reversed: once dreaded as a poison, in the course of time it has changed to a rich storehouse of valuable remedies."

Dr. Hofmann produced a series of lysergic acid derivatives from ergot in 1938. The twenty-fifth in the series was LSD-25, a compound that "aroused no special interest in our pharmacologists and physicians." Testing stopped and LSD was almost lost to the world. For the next five years, Dr. Hofmann worked on other ergot projects, including Hydergine, a treatment for dementia and stroke.

Despite the success of his other research, Dr. Hofmann "could not forget the relatively uninteresting LSD-25," he explained in *LSD, My Problem Child*. In 1943 he again synthesized LSD-25 and, in the process, was overcome by an "unusual sensation." Afterward, he wrote in a note to a colleague:

> *Last Friday, April 16, 1943, I was forced to interrupt my work in the laboratory in the middle of the afternoon and proceed home, being affected by a remarkable restlessness, combined with a slight dizziness. At home I lay down and sank into a not unpleasant intoxicated-like condition, characterized by an extremely stimulated imagination. In a dreamlike state, with eyes closed (I found the daylight to be*

unpleasantly glaring), I perceived an uninterrupted stream of fantastic
pictures, extraordinary shapes with intense, kaleidoscopic play of
colors. After some two hours this condition faded away.

He was unsure how he had become intoxicated. Though the obvious answer was the LSD-25 he had been working with, it seemed odd since he took extreme caution in the lab due to ergot's known toxicity. A very small amount of compound must have come into contact with his skin at some point, he reasoned. If so, it was an incredibly powerful substance. "There seemed to be only one way of getting to the bottom of this," he wrote. "I decided on a self-experiment."

The dizziness and sensation of fainting became so strong at times that
I could no longer hold myself erect, and had to lie down on a sofa. My
surroundings had now transformed themselves in more terrifying ways.
Everything in the room spun around, and the familiar objects and
pieces of furniture assumed grotesque, threatening forms. They were in
continuous motion, animated, as if driven by an inner restlessness.

Even worse than these demonic transformations of the outer world,
were the alterations that I perceived in myself, in my inner being. Every
exertion of my will, every attempt to put an end to the disintegration
of the outer world and the dissolution of my ego, seemed to be wasted
effort. A demon had invaded me, had taken possession of my body,
mind, and soul. I jumped up and screamed, trying to free myself from
him, but then sank down again and lay helpless on the sofa. The
substance, with which I had wanted to experiment, had vanquished
me. It was the demon that scornfully triumphed over my will.

I was aware that LSD, a new active compound with such properties,
would have to be of use in pharmacology, in neurology, and especially

in psychiatry, and that it would attract the interest of concerned specialists. But at that time I had no inkling that the new substance would also come to be used beyond medical science, as an inebriant in the drug scene. Since my self-experiment had revealed LSD in its terrifying, demonic aspect, the last thing I could have expected was that this substance could ever find application as anything approaching a pleasure drug. I failed, moreover, to recognize the meaningful connection between LSD inebriation and spontaneous visionary experience until much later, after further experiments, which were carried out with far lower doses and under different conditions.

Now, little by little I could begin to enjoy the unprecedented colors and plays of shapes that persisted behind my closed eyes. Kaleidoscopic, fantastic images surged in on me, alternating, variegated, opening and then closing themselves in circles and spirals, exploding in colored fountains, rearranging and hybridizing themselves in constant flux. It was particularly remarkable how every acoustic perception, such as the sound of a door handle or a passing automobile, became transformed into optical perceptions. Every sound generated a vividly changing image, with its own consistent form and color.

Exhausted, I then slept, to awake next morning refreshed, with a clear head, though still somewhat tired physically. A sensation of well-being and renewed life flowed through me. Breakfast tasted delicious and gave me extraordinary pleasure. When I later walked out into the garden, in which the sun shone now after a spring rain, everything glistened and sparkled in a fresh light. The world was as if newly created. All my senses vibrated in a condition of highest sensitivity, which persisted for the entire day.

. . .

LSD PROVIDED PASSAGE TO both heaven and to hell. Where it would take a person depended heavily on where that person started from. Initial state of mind and environment set the tone for an acid trip. And for scientists studying the drug, initial assumptions would influence whether a researcher thought LSD was demonic or angelic.

In the United States, initial interest in LSD came from the Central Intelligence Agency, which had been looking for a truth serum that could force enemy spies to divulge classified information. The CIA supported LSD studies starting in the 1950s, and early on, there was optimism. A memorandum from 1954, "Potential New Agent for Unconventional Warfare, LSD," indicated that LSD was useful "for eliciting true and accurate statements from subjects under its influence during interrogation." It became clear, however, that LSD would not always induce true statements—hallucinations and distortions of time and place, among other reactions, could lead to unreliable information.

The CIA did not give up on LSD. After it was found not to be a truth serum, the agency continued to conduct experiments to see if it had other uses. LSD, it was decided, could be useful in confusing and disorienting a subject. Agents could put a subject into an unfamiliar and intimidating environment—such as a fluorescent-lit white lab administered by people in white lab coats—and then threaten to keep the subject drugged and disoriented until they confessed what they knew. "CIA documents," report Martin Lee and Bruce Shlain in *Acid Dreams*, their history of LSD, "indicate that LSD was employed as an aid to interrogation on an operational basis from the mid-1950s through the early 1960s."

The CIA understood LSD psychotomimetically—it thought LSD induced temporary psychosis. "Tripping and psychosis are one and the same," said one agent. "Tripping can be an awful schizoid feeling. Also there are hebephrenics—happy schizos. Their experience is similar to a good trip." When the CIA investigated LSD in sterile labs and under trying conditions, they saw it produce anxiety and insanity. In other contexts, however, LSD had a profoundly different effect.

Psychologists outside of the military and intelligence communi-
ties, such as Dr. Humphry Osmond, were treating patients with LSD
in comfortable apartments and offices. Osmond was a British psychologist interested in psychosis and mental illness. His early work
seemed to show that the hallucinogen mescaline allowed scientists to
understand what schizophrenics experienced—in line with the psychotomimetic view. After later studying LSD's effects on patients,
however, Osmond changed his mind. LSD was not making them crazy,
he concluded.

The novelist Aldous Huxley first tried mescaline under Osmond's
supervision, resulting in a "most extraordinary and significant experience," Huxley later wrote. Mescaline "opens up a host of philosoph-
ical problems, throws intense light and raises all manner of questions
in the field of aesthetics, religion, theory of knowledge." When he
took acid later that year, Huxley had an even more profound experience. Huxley and Osmond disliked the term *psychotomimetic* when
applied to LSD—it assumed the drug was linked to insanity. Their
experiments had shown LSD to be life affirming rather than psychosis inducing, and so they came up with a new term to describe
it—*psychedelic*. Mind manifesting.

"When LSD was first introduced to the United States in 1949, it
was well received by the scientific community," write Lee and Shlain.
"Within less than a decade the drug had risen to a position of high
standing among psychiatrists." A thousand clinical papers concerning
LSD were published, and about forty thousand patients were assessed.
LSD was used to treat alcoholism, autism, and other conditions. It
was found to be neither addictive nor toxic.

LSD also became a popular "mind opener" for people who were
not sick but who desired freedom from society's constricting grip.
These people tended to come from educated and privileged back-
grounds—doctors, artists, writers, actors, students, intelligence agents'
wives—from places that allowed them access to CIA or university
stashes. (Black market LSD became widely available only after LSD

was outlawed.) As LSD became more popular—as people like Huxley and Harvard psychologist Timothy Leary and Beat poet Allen Ginsberg began talking about it publicly—the establishment began to denounce the drug.

Despite backlash from the government, advocates of LSD as a medicine, a mind opener, and a transcendental sacrament prevailed culturally during the sixties. Four million people in North America are thought to have taken LSD in the late sixties, and much of the art, music, and lifestyle that defined the decade—for both those who did and did not use the drug—was influenced by it.

In the decades following the rise of LSD, the drug became weaker and weaker—if not less popular. In the sixties, a typical dose ranged from two hundred to one thousand micrograms. In the nineties, a typical dose was twenty to eighty micrograms. By then, LSD trips were more likely to result in mild euphoria, relaxation, and slightly enhanced visual perception than the full-blown, earth-shattering psychedelic trips encountered in the sixties.

"Strictly speaking," conclude Lee and Shlain, "acid is neither a transcendental sacrament, as Leary claimed, nor an anxiety-producing agent, as initially defined by the CIA and army scientists. Rather, it is a nonspecific amplifier of psychic and social processes." The lasting impression of LSD in the media and in mainstream thinking, however, is of mind wrecker rather than mind opener or simple "nonspecific amplifier." Newspapers, concerned with the growing counterculture, ran splashy headlines about LSD's damning effects throughout the late sixties. The initial CIA view—that LSD caused temporary psychosis—even if unfounded, won out. Those who took the drug were thought to have lost their minds, if only temporarily.

In 1962, Congress and the FDA made it difficult for researchers to obtain LSD. The CIA, which had supported LSD researchers for more than a decade, was becoming less interested in the drug at the time—the agency had mostly moved on to more powerful "super-hallucinogens"—though it still had access to researchers through an

FDA loophole. In 1965 Congress passed the Drug Abuse Control Amendments, which made making and selling LSD a misdemeanor. In 1969, psychedelics, including LSD, were listed as Schedule I Controlled Substances, meaning:

(A) The drug or other substance has a high potential for abuse.

(B) The drug or other substance has no currently accepted medical use in treatment in the United States.

(C) There is a lack of accepted safety for use of the drug or other substance under medical supervision.

41

DROPS OF WATER ARE falling from the branches above me as I climb a dirt path up Mount Davidson. I'm alone on this undeveloped hill in the center of the city. It's early morning, and birds are singing as the sun rises out of sight beyond the fog. The hill is illuminated, but the sun is nowhere to be seen. I walk higher and come to a clearing. The city below is starting to stir. The muffled sound of activity can be heard in the distance.

On the north ridge now, I can just make out a few houses below, behind the fog. Twin Peaks is directly in front of me, but there is no sign of it. The fog is bright white. There is no movement. I turn around and look up the path to the top of the hill. There, the fog is floating around the vine-covered trees. I walk toward it.

The path at the top is wide. Eucalyptus trees, which were brought by immigrants from Australia and then proliferated during the gold rush, stretch above the path. Once again, I hear water droplets falling to the ground. In front of me, rising out of the fog, is a giant concrete cross, 103 feet tall. The cross, like the fog that surrounds it, is white. When the cross was first erected, in 1923, it sat alone on top of the hill, atop the highest point in San Francisco. Eucalyptus grows incredibly fast, and now the cross is veiled by the trees. This morning, it's also veiled by the fog.

Past the cross now, I head down the west side of the hill. Down a small, hidden path and through a torrent of water droplets that fall cold on my skin. There's a small flat area here, in the midst of the swaying trees, and a rock outcropping sits in the middle of it. I stand still on the rocks for a time. I can hear only the soft wind in the trees and the songs of birds around me. The city is now a dull hum washed away by the morning breeze.

The cross on Mount Davidson has slipped out of sight behind me. The sun is rising under the clouds to the east of San Francisco. For a moment, I mistake the sun for a full moon. It looms over the city, a brilliant perfect circle in the early morning sky. I can look right at it. Only when the fog begins to burn off do I realize I've been tricked by my own eyes.

What is seeing?

When I think I see an object, I actually see light bouncing off of the object. I do not see the object itself. It works something like this: Objects absorb light. Not all the light is absorbed, though. Some light bounces off—the mixture of colors that are not absorbed by the object. Each color comes from a particular frequency of light. When I see the white of the cross atop Mount Davidson, I see the mix of colors, or frequencies, that the cross is reflecting, rather than the colors it is absorbing.

When fog comes between me and the cross, I see the fog, not the cross. All light reflected off the cross is deflected by the fog. I can see only the light that is reflected into my eyes by the fog.

My memories are being obscured. Anything remaining to be seen is being deflected somehow. There are still a few things left in Kris's box to look at. No note, though. There is no note.

"A fog that won't burn away drifts and flows across my field of vision," writes Annie Dillard. "When you see fog move against a backdrop of deep pines, you don't see the fog itself, but streaks of clearness floating across the air in dark shreds. So I see only tatters of clearness through a pervading obscurity."

Light is sometimes thought of as particles. Other times, as waves. Different models are useful for different applications. Sometimes it's more useful to think of light as both waves and particles. Quantum optics. Another model.

"I can't distinguish the fog from the overcast sky," writes Dillard, "I can't be sure if the light is direct or reflected. Everywhere darkness and the presence of the unseen appalls."

We make observations of the world constantly. We understand it in models, simplified truths. We speak of facts. I rummage through Kris's box as if I've missed something. Everywhere darkness and the presence of the unseen appalls.

42

43

WHAT A TRAGEDY, INTONE the hushed voices.

Out of an untimely union a child is born. To the south, in another territory. The child is not left to the elements but rather given to a shepherd. The shepherd in turn gives the child to a young and prosperous but childless couple. They raise the child as their own. He loves his new parents. He clings to them fondly.

The child, old enough now to understand, is told that he was born to other parents in another territory. The child's new family loves him. They tell him so. They hold his hand and squeeze it. They could not have a child of their own, they explain, but they were blessed with him.

The child has the advantages of a respected family of sufficient means. He makes friends. He takes an interest in music. He entertains his peers with comical impressions. All along he wonders about his birth, his other family. Why had they given him away?

In time, a younger brother is born. The older child wonders how this could happen, to parents unable to have children of their own. Was it not his fate alone to be their child?

The older child becomes a young man. He yearns to understand the world that created him but did not want him. Where does he belong? Why was he such a burden to his birth parents that he had to be given away? He grows distrustful of his new parents, the only parents he has ever known. He grows distrustful of authority. He argues with fate, which has brought him to his new family. He challenges it.

He is blind to the love of those around him even as he craves love. He yearns for the unseen.

In the final act, the young man, sensitive, intelligent, but with limited vision, hangs himself, like Epicaste, as Homer tells it,

plunging down in a noose from a lofty rafter

. . .

"It's important to remember in a time like this," the eulogist said to the chamber full of friends and family, "that when Kris ended his life it was his response—his responsibility—his choosing."

Why did he choose it? What was the cause of that choice? The drugs? The fear of being caught? How far can we trace the causes? Where did the urge come from, an urge so out of line with the situation?

Kris loved questions. Now we are left with an endless stream of them.

"At the moment of conception, a baby's future is not fully plotted, but some of its general trajectories can be discerned," writes suicide researcher Thomas Joiner, in *Why People Die by Suicide*. "Genes influence neurobiology, including the serotonin system. Genes also influence personality traits like impulsivity, and this influence may occur mostly through genes' impact on the serotonin system. Genetics, neurobiology, and personality all interact in complex ways with an individual's life experience."

What is genetics? What is fate? Should we trace the cause back past Kris? Should we wonder about the birth? About the mother and father? About impulsivity?

Can we see anything clearly?

Sophocles saw blindness well. He took Oedipus's sight for his inability to see. Blindness is universal, we come to believe, in degrees. Had Oedipus a choice in it?

What did we see and when? Writes Sophocles, elsewhere,

Much may mortals learn by seeing;
but before he sees it, none may
read the future or his end.

"Genes, neurobiology, impulsivity, childhood adversity, and mental disorders," writes Joiner, "are interconnected strands that converge and can influence whether people acquire the ability for lethal self-injury, feel a burden on others, and fail to feel that they belong. This lethal endpoint is the culmination of processes started at conception and furthered, biologically and through experience, over a person's lifetime."

We cannot choose our genetic makeup. It is bestowed on us at conception. The double helix, though—we assert—is our architecture but not our fate. We are forever free.

How would we make sense of a world without choice? One where we are led through life by fate?

We choose freedom, and choice, and responsibility. *When Kris ended his life it was his response—his responsibility—his choosing.*

But we cannot be sure. There is no field guide to these matters. Catastrophe, however, seems to find us all at some point. So we warn the living about their choices and say of the dead—in public—that they have chosen. And in private? Of the dead, who no longer have a voice in it, we contemplate genetics and fate, a riddle with no answer.

44

MIRAGES APPEAR AROUND SAN Francisco in the fall. A distant object on the horizon—a ship, say—may appear to float above the sea. Or, even stranger, a ship that's beyond the horizon—in other words, a ship that is out of sight—is somehow visible. Or an object might become vertically distorted: a flat beach in the distance may appear to the viewer as a cliff. Sometimes an object becomes inverted, so that a ship sits upside down above itself, floating both in the sea and sky.

Light travels at different speeds, depending on the density of the air it is traveling through. When it moves from one density to another, the light is refracted—the waves bend—as the light speeds up or slows down. What the viewer sees is a mirage.

A mirage is not a hallucination, it is an optical phenomenon. A hallucination is a mental phenomenon—a compellingly real perception in the absence of an external stimulus.

Common hallucinations include hearing voices; seeing lights, colors, or people who are not there; smelling something that is not present; feeling bodily sensations in a limb that no longer exists. Hallucinations can be caused by psychoactive drugs, by mental illness, by amputation.

"In some cases, hallucinations may be normal," states the National Institutes of Health. "For example, hearing the voice of, or briefly seeing, a loved one who has recently died can be a part of the grieving process."

Sometimes the mind deceives the eyes. The eyes see nothing. The mind inhabits a world all its own.

45

It must be around 4:00 am. I get up and walk to the bathroom in the almost-darkness. I glance into the living room as I walk. Nothing there. I go into the dark bathroom and shut the door.

A popular TV show that Julia and I watch featured a suicide plotline last night. One of the characters, despondent, wakes up in the middle of the night. He goes into the garage where he attaches a garden hose to the exhaust pipe of a car his wife has just bought him—but they cannot afford—and places the other end of the hose in the car through the driver's window. Inside, he tries to start the car but cannot. It will not start. We see the shame on his face. He cannot even do this properly.

He heads to the office, an ad agency on Madison Avenue. It is still night. We see him at his typewriter, writing. The next day he does not show up for work. A woman tries to get into his office, but the door is jammed. She smells a putrid smell. Another character peers into the room. It becomes clear that the man has hung himself, but we do not see the man hanging onscreen. Not at first.

I am back in bed thinking about all this now. Seeing it. I went to sleep easily last night, not thinking too much about the hanging. Now, the dull light of the predawn sun begins to spread out around the edges of the window curtain and I cannot think of anything else.

Several scenes come and go and the man is still hanging in his office—offscreen—as the partners at the agency await the coroner in the break room. Then another partner, the lead, comes into the office. He has been at an early morning meeting and is just now getting to work. The other partners tell him about the man hanging in the other room. The lead insists they cut the man down. There is urgency in his voice and in his movements. His brother had hung himself, in a previous season. Four men struggle to enter the office. They must push aside the hanging man with the door to get in. Inside, we see the man hanging, his skin pale, white, purple. His body stiff. He hangs there as the men look around for something with which to cut him down.

We see him hanging. We cannot escape it. Someone finds something in a desk. Scissors. They grab hold of the dead man and lift him up so that the rope goes slack. One of them saws the rope with the scissors and the dead man falls into the other men's arms. They then lay him out on a couch as if he were sleeping.

The sun is just starting to come up. I get out of bed and go to the living room. The day begins.

46

CERTIFICATION OF VITAL RECORD

STATE OF COLORADO
COLORADO DEPARTMENT OF PUBLIC HEALTH AND ENVIRONMENT
HOLD TO LIGHT TO VIEW WATERMARK

STATE OF COLORADO
CERTIFICATE OF DEATH

STATE FILE NUMBER

DECEDENT

1. DECEDENT'S NAME (First, Middle, Last)	2. SEX	3. DATE OF DEATH (Month, Day, Year)
Kristopher Bryce BOELTE	M	December 16, 1994

4. SOCIAL SECURITY NUMBER	5a. AGE - Last Birthday (Years)	5b. UNDER 1 YEAR Mos. Days	5c. UNDER 1 DAY Hrs. Mins	6. DATE OF BIRTH (Month, Day, Year)	7. BIRTHPLACE (City and State or Foreign Country)
510-86-2495	16			Nov. 6, 1978	Oklahoma City, OK

8. WAS DECEDENT EVER IN U.S. ARMED FORCES? ☐ Yes ☒ No

9a. PLACE OF DEATH (Check only one)
HOSPITAL: ☐ Inpatient ☐ ER/Outpatient ☐ DOA
OTHER: ☐ Nursing Home ☒ Residence ☐ Other (Specify)

9b. FACILITY NAME (If not institution, give street and number)	9c. CITY, TOWN, OR LOCATION OF DEATH	9d. COUNTY OF DEATH
8845 Red Bush Trail	Highlands Ranch	Douglas

10a. DECEDENT'S USUAL OCCUPATION (Give kind of work done during most of working life. Do not use retired)	10b. KIND OF BUSINESS/INDUSTRY	11. MARITAL STATUS - Married, Never Married, Widowed, Divorced (Specify)	12. SPOUSE (If wife, give maiden name)
Student	Student	Never Married	

13a. RESIDENCE-STATE	13b. COUNTY	13c. CITY, TOWN, OR LOCATION	13d. STREET AND NUMBER
CO	Douglas	Highlands Ranch	8845 Red Bush Trail

13e. INSIDE CITY LIMITS? ☒ Yes ☐ No	13f. ZIP CODE 80126	14. WAS DECEDENT OF HISPANIC ORIGIN (Specify No or Yes - If yes, specify Cuban, Mexican, Puerto Rican, etc) ☒ No ☐ Yes Specify:	15. RACE: American Indian, Black, White, etc. (Specify) White	16. DECEDENT'S EDUCATION (Specify only highest grade completed) Elementary or secondary (0 through 12) College (13 through 16 or 17+) 9

PARENTS

17. FATHER-NAME (First, Middle, Last)	18. MOTHER-NAME (First, Middle, Last (Maiden Name))	19. INFORMANT-NAME and relationship to deceased.
Kenneth Boelte	Kathleen Brennaman	Kenneth Boelte- Father

DISPOSITION

20a. METHOD OF DISPOSITION ☐ Burial ☒ Cremation ☐ Removal from State ☐ Donation ☐ Other (Specify)	20b. PLACE OF DISPOSITION (Name of cemetery, crematory, or other place) Englewood Crematory	20c. LOCATION - City or Town, State Englewood, CO

21a. SIGNATURE OF FUNERAL DIRECTOR OR PERSON ACTING AS SUCH WOWoel	21b. NAME AND ADDRESS OF FACILITY: Bullock Mortuary 1375 E. Hampden Av. Englewood, CO ZIP: 80110

22a. REGISTRAR'S SIGNATURE David L Shmitt, Deputy	22b. DATE FILED (Month, Day, Year) DEC 20 1994

CERTIFIER

1 ___
2 ___
3 ___
4 ___
5 ___

23. TIME OF DEATH unknown M	24. DATE PRONOUNCED DEAD Month December Day 16 Year 1994 Hour 7:35 p	25. WAS CORONER NOTIFIED? (Yes or No) yes

TO BE COMPLETED ONLY BY CERTIFYING PHYSICIAN | TO BE COMPLETED BY CORONER

26. To the best of my knowledge, death occurred at the time, date and place, and due to the cause(s) and manner as stated.
Signature ▶

27. On the basis of examination and/or investigation in my opinion death occurred at the time, date and place(s) and due to the cause(s) and manner as stated.
Signature ▶ Mark R Stover

28. DATE SIGNED (Month, Day, Year)

29. DATE SIGNED (Month, Day, Year) Dec 20, 1994

30. NAME, TITLE AND MAILING ADDRESS OF CERTIFIER/CORONER (Type/Print) MARK R. Stover Douglas County Coroner 101 3rd St. CASTLE ROCK ZIP: 80104

31. NAME OF ATTENDING PHYSICIAN IF OTHER THAN CERTIFIER (Type/Print)

CAUSE OF DEATH

32. MANNER OF DEATH ☐ Natural ☐ Pending Investigation ☐ Accident ☐ Undetermined Manner ☒ Suicide ☐ Homicide	33a. DATE OF INJURY (Month, Day, Year) Dec 16, 1994	33b. TIME OF INJURY unknown M	33c. INJURY AT WORK? ☐ Yes ☒ No	33d. DESCRIBE HOW INJURY OCCURRED Hung self from support beam in basement

33e. PLACE OF INJURY-At home, farm, street, factory, office building, etc. (Specify) Home	33f. LOCATION (Street and Number or Rural Route Number, City, County, State) 8845 Red Bush Trail Highlands Ranch Douglas County, CO

34. IMMEDIATE CAUSE (ENTER ONLY ONE CAUSE PER LINE FOR (a), (b), AND (c).) Do not enter mode of dying (e.g. Cardiac or Respiratory Arrest) alone.

PART I

(a) Asphyxiation
DUE TO OR AS A CONSEQUENCE OF

(b) Strangulation by Ligature
DUE TO OR AS A CONSEQUENCE OF

(c)

CONDITIONS IF ANY WHICH GAVE RISE TO IMMEDIATE CAUSE STATING THE UNDERLYING CAUSE LAST

Interval between onset and death
Interval between onset and death
Interval between onset and death

PART II. OTHER SIGNIFICANT CONDITIONS - Conditions contributing to death but not related to cause in PART I (e.g. alcohol abuse, obesity, smoker).

36. AUTOPSY (Yes or No) no	36. IF YES were findings considered in determining cause of death?

DATE ISSUED **JUN 07 2012**

Ronald S. Hyman
RONALD S. HYMAN
STATE REGISTRAR

005881699
REV 01/07

American Bank Note Company

ANY ALTERATION OR ERASURE VOIDS THIS CERTIFICATE

47

PURE BLUE SKIES. MORNING light illuminates the Sunset's white stucco houses. The sea to the west looks calm. The Golden Gate Bridge rises up above the Presidio, solid, its orange once again brilliant against the blue of the sky. The Marin Headlands sit idle beyond the bridge. The view from the fourth floor of the UCSF medical library is spectacular. The library is quiet. A few scattered students sit hunched over books and laptops.

In front of me, *Spitz and Fisher's Medicolegal Investigation of Death*, fourth edition. The book contains many photos I'll probably wish I had never seen. The causes of death are more numerous, more diverse, than could be imagined. Most of us are not accustomed to seeing death. I am not. Like much else in our lives, death is the purview of professionals. Doctors and EMTs and morticians and police. It exists in abstraction.

I turn to chapter XIV, "Asphyxia." The waves crash into Ocean Beach in the distance.

"Asphyxia is a broad term encompassing a variety of conditions that result in interference with the uptake or utilization of oxygen." I keep reading. "A reduced concentration of oxygen in the blood which reaches the brain causes rapid loss of consciousness."

I breathe slowly. I feel my lungs expand with air.

"In all forms of asphyxia, the heartbeat usually continues for several minutes after respiratory arrest. Clinical records suggest that cardiac function may persist for as long as 10 minutes and sometimes longer."

I look up. Out the window at the blue sky. A soft breeze rustles the trees just beyond the windowpane. The sea appears tranquil in the distance. Walk out into the surf and a wilderness awaits. I turn the page.

"Death by hanging usually results from arrest of the arterial blood flow to the brain or obstruction of the venous return, or both."

Hand-drawn illustrations at the bottom of the page show people hanging in various positions. On the facing page, photographs. The next ten pages are full of photographs. Men and women. Young and old. Close-ups of necks abraded. Faces marked by petechiae. Ropes and sheets and cord. From windows and from bedposts. I look at each photo.

"Hanging can be accomplished with the body in any position. The body can be suspended, with feet on the ground, sitting, leaning, even lying down. In the case of *semi-suspension*, arterial blood flow to the head persists while the venous return is interrupted."

The waves begin to come in, one after another.

"Veins are more compressible than arteries. The face is therefore purple, dusky, cyanotic, swollen, sometimes with bulging eyes . . ." The intricacies of death by hanging go on for pages. I read each page.

One paragraph, seemingly out of place in the asphyxia chapter, draws my attention. "We have performed an autopsy of a young man who fell feet first from a height of several stories. At autopsy his intact heart was found in the lower abdomen. The heart apex pierced the diaphragm like an arrowhead." Generally the authors of *Medicolegal Investigation of Death* are not given to extended metaphor. It is a book of blunt facts.

The sky remains clear blue. The waves crash silently. There is no fog. Everything within view is visible.

"Review of all relevant facts suggest that most hangings, whether accidents or suicides, cause a gradual, subtle and painless death."

I spend a morning with the book. Then I place it back on the shelf and move on.

48

THE ELUSIVE GOAL OF fog research is prediction and, somewhat amazingly, prevention. The last paper in my fog stack is a meta-study devoted to the field of understanding fog. "Fog Research: A Review of Past Achievements and Future Perspectives" is, in part, an appeal to others to see the importance of fog and fog research. "The total economic losses associated with the impact of the presence of fog on aviation, marine and land transportation," the authors note, "can be comparable to those of tornadoes or, in some cases, winter storms and hurricanes."

Scientists in such varied fields as meteorology, physical sciences, engineering, medicine, and biology have, the authors note, become increasingly interested in studying fog because it has so much impact on human lives, from aviation to shipping, freshwater supply to commuting.

Prediction is made difficult, despite a large volume of research. The various time and spatial scales create many variables. To start to make predictions, one would need to understand droplet microphysics, aerosol chemistry, radiation, turbulence, surface conditions, and other variables.

My own understanding of the fog is limited. Understanding an action's mechanism is one thing. Predicting that the action will occur at a specific time and place is a very different thing. We live our lives in the present tense, with limited information and complex variables.

....

In the 1970s, fog prevention became a growing area of research. "The main objective of these works was to study how fog can be eliminated from a specific area such as over an airport or a shipping port." Fog droplets are small, just four to ten microns. If you can increase the size of the droplets, you can make the fog coalesce and dissipate. Seeding a fog bank with large dust particles might do the trick. You might also be able to blow the fog away. Helicopters have been used. Imagine all the helicopters hovering over the bay, keeping it clear as the cargo ships come and go. We might rid ourselves of the fog yet.

•   •   •

I AM CONTENT TO stare out at the fog a little longer. "If a thing is worth doing once," painter Mark Rothko said of his later work, "it is worth doing over and over again—exploring it, probing it, demanding by this repetition that the public look at it."

How much fog is enough? How many variations of movement and feeling and composition can there be? How many ways can the wind blow, and tumble, and swirl? How many memories make up a complete story?

Stare into the fog and it is all the same—universal. The mind allows what it will. Each moment is its own particular. Try to capture it, and it is gone. Try to reach into the heart of it; disappear into abstraction. Find meaning in it; become enveloped by it.

"There is no such thing as good painting about nothing," Rothko said.

I haven't seen visions of Kris in a while. Just fog hovering over Twin Peaks to the west.

"A picture lives by companionship, expanding and quickening in the eyes of the sensitive observer," Rothko said. "It dies by the same token. It is therefore risky to send it out into the world. How often it must be impaired by the eyes of the unfeeling and the cruelty of the impotent."

Who sends out this sublime fog? Who takes this risk with us, our lives, the passengers of the SS *City of Rio de Janeiro*? Do we see its beauty as well as its risks?

I've made it through everything in Kris's box. It has lost some of its power in the process. The papers are once again just papers. I've read them all several times now. The letters and notes. The eulogy and death certificate. I've looked through the photographs again and again. I know more than when I first opened it. I feel some relief, even, though the past remains the past and the fog continues to swirl.

It's out there. Walk up this hill and find it. Look over there and see it. Travel this road and know it. Pay no attention and it will creep up on you when the conditions are right. Add up the facts. What is the sum? What have I seen? What have I felt? What else is there to be said? Why try to write it down?

"Silence is so accurate," Rothko said. His life was full. His biography, long. He didn't leave a note.

49

I have forgotten so much.

Today is a clear day. Saturday. The sky outside our living room window is bright blue. Soon, I will head out for a run. I will feel the sun on my skin and look up to the west, toward Twin Peaks, and see the fog rolling in, overflowing into Noe Valley. I will eat lunch first— bread and good cheese and a ripe peach. I will finish another chapter of the book I am reading. Take down a few notes about something I have just learned. Julia will come into the room and I will hold her in my arms, offer a kiss. This is life. The details.

Through it all I carry sadness with me.

It is there, always. Not just Kris now. It has spread out, expanded, opened up. It was born with Kris's death but has dispersed. It is present tense. It awaits moments of significance. Of seeming insignificance. Paint spread across a canvas. An act of kindness. An endless sea of fog.

I think the forgetting has cleansed me. It scares me—the forgetting. I reach out for a memory. It is not there. Memories have been replaced by feeling. Recast, transformed, transfigured.

I reach out. I find one. I hold it close.

Today is clear. Blue skies. And tomorrow—

. . .

I have a memory, a wisp of a memory, of Kris warning me. The memory is associated in my mind with the bathroom we shared. The bathroom that connected our two rooms. I do not see us in the bath-room, talking, as we had a thousand times. Instead, when I think of the memory, I just see the bathroom.

Kris said nothing to me of suicide. In the memory, he says that he is going to do something. The vagueness of his words is ripe with meaning. *Going to do something*. I start to cry. I am crying. I tell him he can't. He sees me crying and he wants to protect me.

He says he won't.

As a teenager, I felt guilty about this memory. I thought, as family and friends of a loved one who dies by suicide often do, that I was guilty in some way. That I knew something. That I could have done something. This wisp of a memory is so thin I now sometimes wonder if it is even real. Did I feel guilty because of the memory or was the memory created by guilt?

At thirteen I knew Kris drank with friends, smoked weed, had sex. What else did I know? What else have I forgotten?

50

THERE IS ONLY WIND. Forever blowing, tearing the sky, screaming past me. I struggle up Eureka Peak. I take a step and brace myself. Take another step and brace myself. I can see only each step as it comes. Past my feet is a vast field of white fog that fades into faint city lights below and darkness above. There is no city, no ocean, no world beyond this wind and fog. I continue up. No one is here. Twin Peaks is empty. There is only this step, and then this step, and then this step.

At the top the wind only gets stronger. I stand and I lean into it. I look out into the emptiness. Fog is everywhere. A perfect fog that has swallowed the world in its sublime embrace. It is fierce, uncompromising. Not much life up here. Not much can live in this relentless wind. And yet, at my feet, reed grass and elderberry cling to the ground.

For a moment, I'm alone and trembling, looking out to the west. I cannot stand here for long, exposed on this peak. I cannot stare out into this fog without being beaten down by the gale pushing against me. I root my legs. I look out at the fog, alone, on top of Twin Peaks.

Out of the white darkness below, Julia comes up the path and appears beside me. She can barely stand without being blown backward. She reaches me and we stand in the wind together. We lean into it, seeing how far we can fall against the sky and still stand. It's too loud to speak. We have to shout to be heard. We smile as we lean further and further into the wind.

We become exhausted and find a space between two large rocks and crouch down between them. The tall reed grass that grows beside the rocks is wet from the residue of the fog. The rocks form a break from the wind but the wind still manages to find us. We sit next to each other, in the midst of it, holding each other. A lone pair of head-lights traces the road around Twin Peaks below the white fog. We pull our hats down lower over our heads.

We sit sheltered between the rocks for a while. After tracing the high-tide line of Ocean Beach together, Julia has walked up here with me. She has been patient with me, this unreasonable search for fog. She has often awoken to an empty space beside her in our bed early in the morning. Watched me sift through papers and artifacts. She has walked beside me at times. She has seen me trembling.

We get up once more. We stand at the top of the peak surrounded by an ocean of noise, the force of the wind, the wet fog. I want to walk over to Noe Peak, to see what it is like over there. It would be darker, farther from the lights. We'd need to climb down the trail to the south and then cross Scenic Drive, past the drivers struggling to see beyond the hoods of their cars. The path drops steeply into the beautiful unseen. We look out into it.

I take a step toward the path but you hold my hand firmly and stand your ground. I look back at you, your hair blowing wildly in the wind, your eyes meeting mine. And I know.

I have seen enough. I have stood directly in the wind. I have faced the fog straight on, been enveloped by it, felt its magnificent embrace. I take you into my arms. I hold you against the violent wind, as you hold me.

This is enough, I think. This peak. This moment.

WITHOUT WHOM

To early readers Victoria, Madeleine, Val, and Jennifer, whose insights were invaluable; to Emily, who allowed me to see some of what she sees; to Della, who brought a poet's eye to bear; to Peter, who was nothing but encouraging and helpful to an unknown writer who ran into him on the street and to whom he owed nothing; to Rolph, for believing; to Richard, who read multiple drafts with enthusiasm; to David, with whom I have wandered and continue to wonder; to Shane, who has been there from the beginning, unfailingly; to Mom and Dad, who never did anything but love us; and to Julia, without whom this book would not exist, nor I, as I am now: thank you.